SCAMS
FROM THE GREAT
BEYOND

How to Make Easy Money Off of ESP, Astrology, UFOs,
Crop Circles, Cattle Mutilations, Alien Abductions,
Atlantis, Channeling, and Other New Age Nonsense

PALADIN PRESS
BOULDER, COLORADO

Scams from the Great Beyond:
How to Make Easy Money Off of ESP, Astrology, UFOs, Crop Circles, Cattle
Mutilations, Alien Abductions, Atlantis, Channeling, and Other New Age Nonsense
by Peter Huston

Copyright © 1997 by Peter Huston

ISBN 0-87364-912-5
Printed in the United States of America

Published by Paladin Press, a division of
Paladin Enterprises, Inc., P.O. Box 1307,
Boulder, Colorado 80306, USA.
(303) 443-7250

Direct inquiries and/or orders to the above address.

Contents

Greetings and Salutations 1

Chapter One

The Glamorous World of the Paranormal 5

PART ONE: PSYCHIC PHENOMENA

Chapter Two

Need Psychic Advice? Call 1-900-PAY-CASH!

Psychic Readings, Telephone Psychics, Predicting the Future,

and the Strange Science of Parapsychology 13

Chapter Three

Mere Entertainers, or Cosmic Vanguards

of a Psychic Master Race?

Telekinesis, and a Few Miscellaneous Tips on Creating a

Reputation as a Psychic 43

Chapter Four

   Can You Hear Me? Can You See Me?

   Hoaxing Telepathy and Clairvoyance 71

PART TWO: UFOs

Chapter Five

   Like Totally Unbelievable Encounters, Dude!

   The Art of Rolling Your Own UFO Photos 91

Chapter Six

   Let My People Go! And While You're At It,

   Keep Off Of My Farm!

   Alien Abductions, Crop Circles, and Cattle Mutilations . . . 113

PART THREE: THE NEW AGE

Chapter Seven

   Suburban Mysticism in 12 Easy Steps!

   The Not Quite So New Age 127

Chapter Eight

   Hi! I'm Pete! Fly Me!

   Meditation Tricks 145

Chapter Nine

Hey, Like Where'd You Learn All This Shit, Anyway?
Establishing a Credible New Age Background 153

Chapter Ten

Hey You! Don't Read the Stars! Read This Book Instead!
Creating an Astrology Column 165

Chapter Eleven

But Seriously Folks 171

Appendix One

Firewalking 177

Appendix Two

Some Periodicals and Organizations of Note 181

Bibliography 187

Greetings and Salutations

"You're not a fucking folk hero! You're just a goddamn psychopath!"

—Wynona Ryder in the motion picture *Heathers*

In 1729, Jonathan Swift, political satirist and author of the classic *Gulliver's Travels*, caused a stir. The English, it seems, were exploiting their Irish neighbors. The Irish were left overworked and underfed, and their children were starving. As this was in the days long before the introduction of birth control, the Irish had large families, generally larger than they could afford. Thousands upon thousands of Irish babies would die of starvation, malnutrition, and ill care each year. Meanwhile, their rich, overfed English landlords stood by and did nothing.

Swift wrote his classic piece, *A Modest Proposal,* in which he pointed out that the situation was tragic and pointless. When the babies died, as they constantly did, the Irish suffered and the English gained nothing. He stated, with a perverse sort of logic, that if the English overlords were to purchase the children from their parents for a small sum, then roast and eat them as the main course of a banquet, the children would be just as dead, but the Irish peasants would at least gain some money for their troubles, and the English landlords, on their side, would gain an elegant meal.

Of course, what Swift hoped to do was to shock the people of his time into taking action to correct a horrible and unjust economic situation. Instead, few understood, and Swift was vilified, insulted, and subjected to a wide range of personal attacks and slander.

In this book, I don't advocate cannibalism, but I do advocate theft, swindling, fraud, and the manipulation of one's fellow human beings in order to obtain personal gain. If you'd like, you may respond by working to educate people, promote critical thinking, and create a society where the bulk of the population is informed enough to use the basics of science, logic, and reason to evaluate situations and then be able to use their minds to protect themselves and others from the swindlers, cultists, and con men whose goals are to lie, trick, rob, and control them using claims of the miraculous.

Or, if you'd prefer, you may vilify, insult, and slander me. The choice is yours. For now, though, I simply hope this work makes enough of an impression to be memorable.

Thanks are in order for assistance with this work. As always, assistance does not always indicate agreement with the author— often quite the contrary. Let's begin with the usual band of suspects. Mark Shammon advised me on the use of the word processor and proved himself to be a highly qualified "New Age Consultant." Without him this work would most likely be a giant glitch sitting on a computer disk somewhere inside this convoluted machine. Dr. Robert Baker, author and psychologist, provided a great deal of assistance in recommending reading materials and helping me find some virtually impossible-to-obtain, out-of-print materials that were of great help. James Randi, world famous skeptic, conjurer, entertainer, and author, was generous in offering difficult-to-impossible-to-obtain information. Joe Nickell, author, conjurer, and investigator, took time out from his busy schedule to offer invaluable assistance in obtaining some of the effects described in this work. I promise readers that if they like this work, and perhaps even if they don't, they will benefit by reading the many fine works of these great educators. Also, please keep in mind that the final form and flavor of the work is mine alone. They provided advice. I provided the humor and tone.

Carolyn Touchette, Grace Huston, my mother and father, Robin Huston, and Eric Krauter assisted in a variety of ways. Megan Touchette and Lewis Treadway proved themselves able and willing photographic assistants. Zhao Jie volunteered, as well, but just couldn't make it on the day scheduled. Donald Krauter generously provided photographic advice. Kelsey Touchette stayed out of the way and behaved herself. It's my fondest hope that someday, when she's bigger, she'll assist in a future project.

The members of the Inquiring Skeptics of Upstate New York assisted a whole big bunch. Therefore, in no particular order, let me thank the following: Michael Sofka, Karla Sofka, Barry Haines, Daniel Forrest, Ken Meyers, and all the rest. Daisy the spastic dog gave up a chew toy for this valuable project. Maria Perry of the Flights of Fantasy Bookstore in Albany, New York, took many strange special orders. Border's Books and Music of Colonie, New York, did the same when she needed a break. The Capital District Discount Hobby Center gave me a great deal on the Testor's UFO kit. Owl Pen Books in Cambridge, New York, assisted with the occasional out-of-print book search. The folks at Photo Images in Glenville, New York, cheerfully handled some very strange requests as to the processing of rolls of film and did so without blinking. The staffs of various New Age bookstores in Boston and the New York Capital District assisted quite generously. Barry Karr of the incomparable Committee for the Scientific Investigation of Claims of the Paranormal (CSICOP) in Buffalo, New York, assisted, although he is most certainly much too polite and gentile to be held responsible for the caustic tone of the present work. The folks at Huntington House, a Christian book publisher, should also be thanked for contributing a pair of their works to a previous project of mine. These works have now found their way into the bibliography of this volume.

The many fine folks involved in *Skeptical Inquirer* magazine, especially Ken Frazier and Paul Kurtz, and its competitor, Michael Shermer and *Skeptic*, must be thanked for making so much of this information available. It's hoped that they approve or at least understand the purpose of the present work. Thanks to Jon Ford of Paladin Press for approving such a project in the first place and giving me yet another chance to shoot my mouth off in public. A frightening number of publishers refuse to touch skeptical works concerning the paranormal for fear that, if well done, they might hurt sales in their New Age and Occult lines. The end result is that this important subject is represented in a way to promote profits rather than truth in far too many bookstores throughout the world. Fortunately, we live in a country where alternatives to giant corporate publishers still exist.

I'd like to thank all those Niskayuna High School English teachers who kept threatening to fail me time and time again, giving me straight Cs and Ds throughout tenth and eleventh grade, on this the occasion of the release of my second book. Now it's your turn to find the symbolism and deeper meaning within it!

Finally, various "psychics," "chi kung masters," "channelers," and others donated or sold time to make this book what it is. I couldn't have done it without you guys.

Best wishes. God bless us everyone!

Peter Huston
Schenectady, New York

The Glamorous World of the Paranormal

The pilgrim climbed the mountain, led forward by his quest. One weary footstep to the next, his goal remained the same. Knowledge. Wisdom. The chance to meet the great guru of the mountain. The legendary wise man who sat at the top of the craggy peak. The one whose otherworldly abilities and powers were legend far and wide.

Hour upon hour. Day upon day. Through snow, hail, and rock slides, the seeker climbed. Thoughts of the one with the mythical powers fixed on his mind like a magnet, pulling him forward. The icy mountain cold tore straight through the thin cloth of his pilgrim's robes, leaving him no more sheltered than a naked man. Yet he continued forward. His heart beat with anticipation of the secrets the master could teach him.

And then, one day, it came to pass. The epic encounter he'd dreamed of for so long became reality. As he trudged forward in *the thin air of the narrow, treacherous path, he rounded the final bend. In front of him was the man renowned as the great guru of the mountain, the man with the mythical powers, known far and wide for his supernatural talents.*

The guru sat on a folding chair leaning back holding a cold bottle of Miller, a brew known far and wide for its low price at all major convenience stores. Dressed in old jeans, a hooded sweatshirt, and torn-up sneakers, his attention was clearly focused on a bad kung fu movie that he watched on a small battery-powered television set. His hair was disheveled, his face relaxed, and his clothing bedraggled.

He turned, looked the weary pilgrim full in the face, and reached for a sauce-covered chicken wing from a large bowl next to his chair. "Hi! Want one?" he said, addressing the tired traveler . . .

Most people have some sort of belief in something that they would consider supernatural, unexplained, or paranormal. Such beliefs are so overwhelmingly common and prevalent throughout such a wide variety of cultures that many would say that having these beliefs is one of the things that makes us human. Within us all there exists a yearning to believe in something greater, more exciting, and more glamorous than our own often mundane existence. And, sadly, when people have a strong yearning for something, then others can use this desire to manipulate and trick them.

There exists a large market for the miraculous, and naturally so, for who would not like to see a miracle? Yet few informed people can deny that the bulk of this market is fed by frauds. This work is intended as an introduction to some of the methods by which miraculous powers can be simulated or fraudulent "evidence" of a supernatural or otherworldly happening can be created. By familiarizing oneself with the methods of the hoaxers and con men, one can begin to look at unexplained phenomena in a new light.

Whether such phenomena as described have any basis in fact lies outside the scope of this small book. If forced to give an answer, I would state that I do not believe in the reality of the phenomena that I discuss, yet many would simply dismiss me as a cynic.

Nevertheless, it is these very people, the believers, who should find this work the most valuable. These are the people most vulnerable to being hoaxed and manipulated by unscrupulous con artists.

Many readers will be tempted to try out some of the techniques described in this book. A warning may be in order. Although some of these ideas seem so out of the ordinary that the thought of using them sounds harmless, there is a very real potential for tragedy. People are often surprisingly willing to accept the most outrageous things as being true. If you play with people's ideas of reality, then you have created a dangerous situation. Such pranks can easily get out of hand, so if you must try them, use forethought and be careful.

Some acceptable uses for the techniques shown are:

1. To entertain and amaze people.
2. To make the world more interesting.
3. To educate people about just how easy it is to fake certain things.
4. To better understand and reevaluate many of the claims regarding the paranormal made by parts of the media and certain individuals and groups.

Nevertheless, there are quite a few people out there who wish to utilize techniques such as those shown in this book to defraud others into thinking that they are someone they are not. Having done this, they often then use people to acquire wealth and power. Unacceptable uses of these techniques are:

1. To convince people that you truly have otherworldly powers. Often in such a situation, the fraud's true goal is to create a dependent type of relationship. The alleged psychic (or fortune-teller, tea-leaf reader, past-life therapist, phrenologist, or what have you) will seek to convince his "clients" (or, in con man's terminology, "marks") that he is particularly endowed with otherworldly insight. He will share this insight and

help the clients with all of their problems . . . for a fee, of course.

Although this sort of dependency is unsettling and disturbing, what makes it worse is that in some cases, "psychics" have convinced other individuals to devote large portions of time, money, and emotional energy to things that they would not normally do were it not for misplaced belief in the psychic's phony powers.

2. Running seminars or even starting a full-time school, "research center," or "retreat" to teach others the powers you only pretend to have. Of course, it's all right to teach people skills that you know, and it's generally fair to accept some sort of compensation for it. It is, on the other hand, completely immoral to promise to teach students something that you can't deliver.

Some people have made money with courses that offer to teach individuals marvelous powers. When the students fail to acquire these powers, they are often told that it is their own fault, as they either lack talent or perseverance. In other cases, the deceived students are kept on by being told they are close to success and should stick with it a little while longer, for the usual tuition, of course. In most cases, when students recognize such schools for the scams that they are, some flimsy excuse is used to deflect blame from where it should lie—the teacher's own fraudulent nature. In some of the most peculiar and disturbing examples of such things, the students actually brainwash themselves into believing that they have the powers they have been "taught."

3. Make a career out of hoaxing gullible believers with your "powers." In the past, many magicians, including Harry Houdini, Joseph Dunninger, James Randi, David Hoy, and George Kreskin, have marketed themselves as having "real abilities." [1] In the bulk of these cases,

such people have ultimately found that they are better off marketing themselves truthfully as entertainers who use conjuring techniques and illusion to simulate spectacular effects. Not only do they get the credit that they deserve for the talents that they have, but they don't need to maintain an act when the show's over. They can be who they want to be and discuss their true art—creating illusions—openly, without the strain of having to live a life of self-imposed false mumbo-jumbo and make-believe mysticism.

It is widely believed by many magicians that many, if not all, of the world's prominent psychic performers are simply using the same sorts of techniques that they use while simply hiding the fact from the public.

4. Start a cult. Although I support freedom of religion, it is shameless when a person knowingly creates a religious group simply so that he or she may control other people. Yet it happens all the time.

If you are thinking of starting a cult, before you do so, at the very least give the project some serious thought. Initially, perhaps, the thought of having a group of people surrounding you, treating you as a god, and obeying your every whim and command, no matter how strange or bizarre, may sound appealing. But the full effects are not so nice. These people, your followers, won't leave you alone. Furthermore, they don't really want to know "you." They just want to spend time with the godlike being you pretend to be. Having a group of people hanging on your every word might sound good at first, yet hour after hour, day after day, year after year of this sort of thing begins to change a person. Look at such "successful" cult leaders as David Koresh or Jim Jones. These guys had large numbers of followers who were quite ready and willing to die for them upon command. Yet, by the time their careers ended in widespread death and destruction, they had both become so kooky that they eagerly died completely pointless deaths. Charles Manson, another "successful" cult leader, is locked up with little real chance of parole. Other examples could be cited.

The entire psychology behind even the most bizarre cults is that although the members' behavior is quite strange to the outside world, when judged by the standards of their fellow cultists, it seems quite normal. Over time, in many cases this internal standard within the group changes, little by little becoming progressively more bizarre. The leader's behavior often shifts right along with it. [2] Do you really think that you are strong enough to remain sane when surrounded exclusively by kooks who fully believe in some completely nonsensical set of delusions that you knowingly created on a whim, without the opportunity of even a vacation from your self-appointed, full-time role as messiah and omniscient all-father?

Don't start cults! It's bad karma, and the entire idea will probably bounce back in your face and make you miserable and insane sooner or later. You will regret it someday if you do.

People who create and hoax a wide variety of paranormal and psychic phenomena for entertainment purposes are known as magicians, or, as they prefer to be called, conjurers. The division between magicians and fraudulent wonder workers is that the first group are creating illusions, the second group are living a lie.

Nevertheless, if you wish to join the ranks of the scum who use such techniques to deceive, then there's no overwhelming reason why you can't be the next New Age guru or fraudulent psychic. The requirements are simple. First, you'll need a sociopathic outlook on life and the ability to lie easily. Second, you'll need the techniques in this book. Beyond that, there's little else needed. The paranormal enthusiasts will provide the rest.

ENDNOTES

1 Neher, *The Psychology of Transcendence,* p. 223.

2 See Galanter, *Cults, Faith, Healing, and Coercion,* for details.

Part 1
PSYCHIC PHENOMENA

Need Psychic Advice? Call 1-900-PAY CASH!

Psychic Readings, Telephone Psychics, Predicting the Future, and the Strange Science of Parapsychology

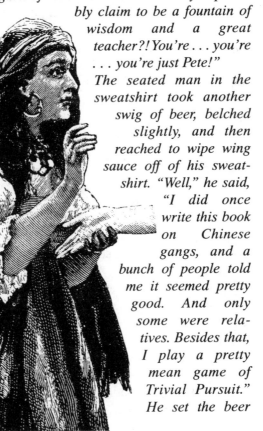

The pilgrim's jaw dropped and his eyes glared angrily. "But you can't be the great guru of the mountain! How can you possibly claim to be a fountain of wisdom and a great teacher?! You're . . . you're . . . you're just Pete!"

The seated man in the sweatshirt took another swig of beer, belched slightly, and then reached to wipe wing sauce off of his sweatshirt. "Well," he said, "I did once write this book on Chinese gangs, and a bunch of people told me it seemed pretty good. And only some were relatives. Besides that, I play a pretty mean game of Trivial Pursuit." He set the beer *down on the ground, reached for another gooey wing, returned his attention to the kung fu movie, and smiled.*

The pilgrim spit on the ground in disgust. "That has nothing to do with anything! I trudged all the way up this mountain seeking enlightenment! If you don't show me some supernatural abilities, some untapped human potential right this second, then . . . then . . . I'll kick your goddamn bottle of beer right over!"

"Whoa! Hold on. There's no need for beer spilling. Heavens! Now sit down."

The pilgrim sat as he'd been trained long ago: legs carefully crossed in a full lotus position, left heel on the right knee, right heel on the left knee. "Am I ready, great guru?"

"Sure, that'll do I guess," said the teacher. Then suddenly, the guru shifted his appearance. His visage became mystical. "My child, the fates tell me that if you abandon your path, you will learn nothing of what you seek. Yet, if you continue with the pilgrim way, keeping your mind open and your heart pure, the future has much wisdom to show you. For I can see, with my psychic reading, that you are eager, ready to learn, and clearly able to discern what is true and what is false when it comes to matters of the spirit."

"Ah yes," sighed the student contentedly. He sat attentively, eager to learn all he could of the art of reading the future and the nature of a man's spirit . . .

Among much of the general public, there's a belief that psychic powers and ESP (extra sensory perception) have been accepted by the scientific community based on hard evidence produced in carefully controlled experiments. When I learned that, sadly, this was not the case, I admit I was quite disappointed. Since a belief in psychic phenomena is very strong in our society (in fact, a belief in having superpowers of all sorts recurs again and again throughout human history), it is worth spending some time on why exactly most scientists don't take the possibility of such powers too seriously.

Simply put, one problem is that a requirement for a successful scientific experiment is repeatability. For example, if one chemist gets a particular result for a particular experiment, then all the other chemists in the world need to be able to repeat the experiment under similar conditions and achieve a similar, if not identical, result. This is important. Not only does it allow a high school chemistry teacher to check and see if his or her students are doing the experiment correctly, but it also allows for one chemist to double-check another.

With parapsychology (the name for the science of studying psychic phenomena), this sort of verifiability simply hasn't happened. Although some scientists have done some very interesting and exciting experiments that seem to show that humans have some telepathic ability, the majority of researchers have not been able to repeat these experiments and achieve the same or similar results. Either psychic powers are fickle and unreliable or else the experiments were poorly designed.

Some magicians have been quick to point out the many opportunities for cheating during the experiments and argue that because of this, the tests prove nothing. "There's no such thing as psychics," argue the skeptics, "just cheaters."

This being the case, well then, *let's cheat!* Over the remaining chapters, a variety of cheating methods will be shown and described. If you'd like, you may then infiltrate parapsychology laboratories and produce mayhem and confusion to your little heart's delight with your very own Project Alpha. [1] (If anybody asks, by the way, we don't mean this. We're only joking, and this book is presented for academic and entertainment purposes only.)

After all, if psychic phenomena do not really exist, then we will just have to improvise and create some. Remember, television needs psychics! *Star Trek, Babylon Five, Doctor Who,* and all those other really groovy shows love the use of untapped psychic powers as an occasional plot device. There's even an entire genre of annoying, goofy pseudo documentaries with titles like *Bizarre Filmings, Outings, Unexplained Mysteries, Already Explained Mysteries, Unexplained as of Yet Mysteries,* and *Marginally Mysterious Mysteries.* Surely the truth is a small sacrifice indeed, just so long as we can be assured a steady stream of shows such as this!

But there's more than just television and flimsy scientific tests. Ordinary people often find what they believe to be intuitively convincing evidence, such as a well-done psychic reading. During a psychic reading, a "psychic" uses his or her alleged powers to examine a subject and "read" him. They then tell the person all about himself and his future. Generally speaking, a psychic giving a reading often includes advice and generalizations about problems to the client. Many clients feel that due to the seemingly great insight that the psychic has into their lives, their personality, and their situation, a good reading serves as proof of the psychic's powers. Psychic readings traditionally take place in person, although there is an increasing amount of money to be made by telephone psychics, who, as the name indicates, give readings over the phone. All in all, a psychic reading is virtually identical to a traditional fortune-telling session seen in many cultures.

In this chapter we will teach you the essentials of how to give convincing psychic readings, whether you have psychic powers or not. You may then, if you'd like, trick people, lie to them, and, in short, rip them off.

Let's start with a brief background. As stated, a "psychic advi-

sor" is, in effect, a glorified fortune-teller under another name. If you have any doubts about this, just watch an infomercial or two for phone psychics. You'll see the alleged psychics pull out Tarot cards, make astrological references, advocate reincarnation, describe auras, sense guardian angels, and, in short, do everything that a classical fortune-teller is supposed to do (but a true psychic would have no need for) short of reading signs in the wriggling entrails of a recently sacrificed goat. (The American public, it seems, disapproves of gore.)

But logic has no part in the psychic reading. Note the adds for psychic astrologers reproduced throughout this chapter. What is a psychic astrologer, anyway? Aren't psychic phenomenon and astrology two different things? Kind of like plumbers and electricians? Or cooks and garbagemen? Or models and waitresses? Nevertheless, illogical as they may be, claims of psychic astrologers, like the Whopper Junior and low-fat "lite" potato chips, seem to be here to stay, and the only hope for the world and our collective sanity is for you, the reader, to buy as many copies of this book as you can possibly afford and pass them out on street corners to strangers and passersby! Maybe, just maybe, by doing so you can knock a little sense into someone who desperately needs it. But . . . back to the subject.

Why would anyone consult a psychic reader? The reasons vary. Some, of course, are simply seeking cheap thrills and entertainment, and although this could be expensive, few would argue that it is necessarily harmful. Others are hardworking people with real troubles and difficulties. Such people are seeking the same things that we all seek when we are under stress—reassurance, help with decisions, and caring attention. The safest and easiest way for the fortune-teller, psychic reader, and psychic astrologer to give them this and guarantee a satisfied client is to simply listen carefully and let them know that they are doing so.

There's a technique for this. Psychotherapists and crisis intervention workers are trained in it, and a good fortune-teller instinctively knows how to do it as well. It's called "active listening." A typical active-listening exchange goes something like this:

Troubled Person: "I'm troubled."
Active Listener: "So you feel that you're troubled . . ."
Troubled Person: "Yes, I feel that I have many problems."
Active Listener: "So, you feel that you have many problems . . ."
Troubled Person: "That's right."
Active Listener: "Could you tell me more?"
Troubled Person: "My mother tells me it's a shame that I write for Paladin Press instead of looking for a real job."
Active Listener: "So, you feel that your mother thinks it's a shame that you write for Paladin Press instead of looking for a real job . . ."

And so on and so forth. Astute readers will have quickly noted that the active listener is focusing his attention on the statements of the troubled person and contributing little to nothing new to the conversation. This is exactly the way that active listening is designed to proceed. A skilled and well-trained psychotherapist will often use active listening as a way to elicit more information before proceeding into a more curative form of therapy. A less-trained (but perhaps equally dedicated) psychotherapy provider, such as a hot line volunteer, will use this method as part of giving psychological first aid and calming reassurance before referring a truly needy person elsewhere for more definitive treatment.

Although such a system of communication sounds silly or obvious to a calm and collected outsider, often a troubled person is simply quite relieved to have finally found a place to release his pent-up emotions and unburden himself and his problems in the assurance that someone, at last, really is listening.

To truly troubled people, such attention from a caring person is often all that they need to collect themselves and get their heads together before they choose a course of action for dealing with their problem (and such action may or may not involve psychotherapy). A skilled fortune-teller can provide this, and in some cultures this is seen as a very real part of their services. The risks of such an approach will be detailed later.

A second service that can be offered in such circumstances is advice, the vaguer the better. Now, in the psychotherapeutic professions there are a great many ethical and legal constraints placed on what sorts of advice can be offered to a client and what cannot. Generally speaking, only in the most extreme cases can a hot line volunteer or emergency service worker give real recommendations to needy people (e.g., "Don't jump! Come to the hospital first!"). There are reasons for this.

Although some psychotherapists are, of course, manipulative, they do at least belong to professions and associations where uneth-

ical behavior is supposed to be monitored and punished. Unscrupulous fortune-tellers and predatory so-called psychics are normally unlicensed and don't need to follow such guidelines. They are free to give advice any way they choose. "Leave your husband." "Sell the farm." "Stop writing for Paladin Press and get a job plucking chickens." These are all examples of valid advice in some, but not all cases, although there is no guarantee that the alleged psychic is qualified to determine when.

In some cases, fortune-tellers, psychics, and psychic astrologers take advantage of their power to manipulate a patient. As I write this, a local "paranormal enthusiast" who claimed supernatural powers has recently been sent to prison. [2] Among the allegations are that he gave advice to 15-year-old girls that included, "I think it would help if you had sex with me," and "I think it would be good for you if, from time to time, you gave me a jar of your urine for me to drink." According to newspaper and police claims, the girls actually did these and other

things that the psychic is said to have requested before they wised up, stopped satisfying his fetishes, and contacted authorities.

There are cases on record of gypsy fortune-tellers giving credulous clients advice such as, "Your money has been cursed. Hand it over to me and I will remove the curse for you before giving the money back." At this point, on multiple occasions such con artists have then absconded with the money and fled the state, never to be seen again. [3]

Convincing clients that one has psychic powers can be done in several ways, and phony psychics rely on several factors to achieve the desired effect. One of the most important is the so-called "Barnum effect." Named after P.T. Barnum of Barnum and Bailey Circus fame, this hinges on the fact that if you attempt to convince people that you can tell fortunes, most of them will want to assist you in making them believe in your powers. Encourage this. Enlist their aid. Magicians and others have developed a "classic reading" (see Addendum 2-1 at the end of this chapter). Most people, unfamiliar with the reading, will feel that it describes them to a T.

Of course it works better if you can tell people something about themselves that you aren't supposed to know. A skilled fortune-teller is trained in "cold reading," another magicians' technique. With cold reading, the psychic begins making predictions in a rather vague manner but focuses in on more specific statements as he watches for cues from the subject. Watch the psychic hot line infomercials some night if you want to see how this is done. The psychic will begin by saying, "I'm getting a strong impression of children. You often spend time around children," or something equally vague and then gradually hover in on, "I feel that maybe you have children of your own. Perhaps two or three children. All of young ages," until finally the subject chortles out in glee, "That's amazing! I have a little girl and a little boy who are 6 and 8 years old!"

There are several ways to do this. The simplest—and the telepsychics do this all the time—is to simply ask the test subject how they're doing. "Am I close?" "Does that sound right to you?" and "What do you think?" are all common cues and blatant requests for feedback. To an observer it can almost seem that the client and the reader are playing some kind of strange parlor game based on guessing one another's personality. ("I sense a problem. How am I doing?" "Good. You're probably sensing my dog's illness. It's been worrying me.") If one happens to be a palm reader, then you can also hone in on the muscle tension, reflexive movements, or lack thereof that you feel in the person's muscles as you "read" his palm. A good fortune-teller tries to turn the client into a participant in the experience.

You cannot go wrong by paying too much careful attention to body language. Remember that when a person agrees with what you are saying and is interested, they will generally move closer and relax. If they disagree with what you are saying or feel uncomfortable, then they will tend to stiffen up and lean away. You can obtain invaluable clues from watching a person's body. [4]

But don't just watch what a person does with his body. Examine his body itself. For example, you can often get some idea of how a person lives and what sort of work he is in if you inspect his hands for callouses. Income can be determined by clothes, jewelry, or shoes. Hairstyle and attentiveness to grooming, as well as fashion sense, wedding rings, make-up and cosmetics, manicures, fingernail polish or lack thereof, and perfumes or colognes or lack thereof, and so on can teach you large amounts about the person and his or her relationships and attitudes toward dating, romance, possible love life, and so on. Clearly the clothes that people choose to wear reveal a great deal about their attitudes toward fashion trends and how they respond to such trends. (An extreme example is that body piercing is "hip" in some counterculture circles but not tolerated where conservative corporate conformity is stressed. I, on the other hand, do not have pierced body parts, but on most days it is fairly obvious from my virtually worn-out jeans and comfortably beaten-in shoes that I do not belong to the corporate subculture.)

Make note of religious and other personal symbols. Some people, for example, like to advertise their affiliation with a given organization or group of people, such as the military or a volunteer fire department. But don't just comment on their affiliation. It's too obvious, and it might even be placed there to throw you off. It would probably be best to comment instead on the underlying attitudes and traits that the person wishes to project by advertising their affiliation. For example, with both volunteer firemen and the military, their perceived bravery is an important trait that they probably like to advertise.

Other facts that can help you falsify a proper psychic reading include the subject's apparent age; if they have a wedding ring and the apparent age and cost of the ring, particularly if you compare it to their current clothes (e.g., a cheap ring that's several years old combined with expensive clothes indicates that a person has had a gain in income since they were married); did they come alone to the reading and, if not, who accompanied them; level of physical fitness, muscularity, and type of muscularity (e.g., people who work in a job with heavy lifting are often strong but overweight, while health spa junkies tend to develop a totally different sort of figure). Combine this information with friendly and subtle requests for feedback and you're already halfway there to a good psychic reading.

On the telephone one must rely on auditory rather than visual cues. A great deal about a person's approximate age, intelligence, ethnic background, level of education, place of origin, state of health, emotional state, social class, and so forth can be determined by their voice, vocabulary, and use of language. [5]

A good psychic pumps the listener for as much information as he possibly can. For example, the subject may be told that the psychic needs his exact birthday and astrological sign or those of people near him to test for interactions. The caller may even be asked to give a description of why they called. (Hmmm, I thought this was the psychic's job? And come to think of it, like the old joke says, if they're so psychic, why don't they call *you* when you're having a problem?)

Clever application of statistics can help. Good magic shops carry manuals on cold reading. One of these, which I own, is simply full of interesting facts, such as "78% of adults have aches or problems associated with their feet, more for women who wear high heeled shoes," or "Young girls usually think about nursing and teaching. Young boys think about becoming an animal trainer" or "Nearly every adult has lost someone close to them, separated by death or divorce."[6]

Imagine the impression that you would make on a middle-aged woman who you had just met by combining these statements: "Despite having worked hard for all your life, you have still maintained your essential goodness. Even as a little girl you felt a strong need to care for others and were drawn toward helping others. You dreamed of becoming a nurse or a teacher. You've worked hard, sometimes so hard that you feel an actual physical aching in your feet or back. Sometimes you miss someone close who is now gone from your life. There will be difficult times ahead, but you will get through them just as you've found the strength within yourself to persevere through other difficult times." If she works with you, even going so far as trying to determine the source of the references that you are making or adding detailed information to your vague descriptions ("Why you must be talking about Uncle Charlie's pet iguana Starchie!"), chances are she'll walk away convinced.

Notice the way the client is subtly praised, complimented, and encouraged during the reading. It doesn't take psychic powers to know that most people feel tragically underappreciated by those around them. This praise alone is enough to keep the client coming back in many cases.

If the person looks amazed and surprised when you detect something accurate, remember to say "the feeling is now growing much stronger. Yes, I can feel it quite clearly." As with everything else in life, practice makes perfect, and don't forget to work with the person's natural inclinations.

Before making any questionable statements, be sure to preface them with a bit of uncertainty, such as, "I don't know what it means, but I'm getting a feeling that you . . ." or, "Maybe, just maybe, there's a slight impression coming to me that . . ." If the client gives a negative response, stating that they have never "had even the least bit of difficulty dealing with authority" (although most adults have some trouble) or they "do not like attending flea markets in the least" (many mature women do), then you can easily back out of the situation. If prefaced properly, such minor misstatements can be explained away as a "psychic echo" or "telepathic bleeding from a nearby person or entity." ("Happens all the time to a powerful psychic, such as myself. Quite annoying, too," you might say.)

If the client continues to disagree with what you are saying, then sometimes you can convince him that either he is in denial or simply doesn't understand his own feelings, but this is overbearing and doesn't always work. Avoid it. Instead, tell him you're precognitive and "Although these may not be your feelings at present, they will almost certainly become this way at some point in the future." If this is too extreme or you wish to modify his behavior, then change this to, ". . . at some point in the future if present trends continue." You should always be prepared to tack on such statements if the client begins grimacing or looking at you as if you are completely wrong. By doing this you quickly shift your statement from the present to a possible future. And after all, who are they (the client) to claim to know all possible futures? If they were psychic, then they wouldn't be wasting their time coming to you, now would they?

And finally, if all else fails, cheat! That's right, cheat. Don't hesitate to spy on people. Ask their friends, co-workers, and mutual acquaintances all about them if you get the chance. Look up things in local newspapers and county records. Do a full background check on them. If you have a friend in the Department of Motor Vehicles, get ahold of their driving record, professional licenses, and all other public records that will help you learn about this person.

If this still isn't enough, then offer to swap information on clients with your fellow fraudulent psychics. In Lamar Keene's classic and sadly long out of print work, *The Psychic Mafia,* he describes how fraudulent spirit mediums such as himself often knew one another and worked in concert, keeping extensive files and exchanging pieces of information on wealthy clients in order to assist one another.

According to Keene, the effect on a client was simply astonishing when he offered them information that he "could not possibly have acquired through Earthly means," such as the name of their long-deceased son, particularly when combined with a piece of trivia such as their son's love of swimming and a bland message such as, "He loves you, says hello from the spirit world, and hopes that you are doing well and not worrying too much about your garden."

(Keene's exposé, by the way, caused enough of a sensation that he was shot and wounded in his driveway one night, possibly by someone connected with the sort of mediums who he had been skewering and whose techniques he described in the book. Keene ultimately recovered. [7])

It should also be mentioned that if you can tie up with a celebrity client, particularly a slightly flaky movie star like Shirley Mac-Laine, then you are sure to do well. Not only will such a person give you great publicity, but so much of their so-called "private life" is on public record that you can learn an incredible amount about them simply by digging through old piles of moldy tabloids. Prominent politicians and world leaders are another great catch.

Don't laugh. Ronald Reagan's schedule was determined for a considerable length of time by his wife Nancy based on behind-the-scenes consultations with her astrologer. And for our good friends up north in Canada, former long-time prime minister William Lyon MacKenzie attended seances, where he spoke to the spirits of his deceased dog and mother, and was frequently advised by mediums. [8]

Let's see what happens when you put it all together. A couple of years ago, an acquaintance of mine visited a psychic at the urging of some of her co-workers. It was, in effect, a group office outing. The psychic told her she'd lost someone close to her recently, someone unexpected perhaps. This person was quite surprised and quickly agreed. Someone young. My friend promptly said that she was probably referring to a suicide victim who had been a friend of her family. The psychic responded, "His spirit is looking out for you." By this time my friend was hooked. The psychic then told her that her three-year-old daughter would become quite talented, probably either in music or athletics. Naturally, any mother would love to hear this, and this one was no exception. To believe means that her child is prophesied for greatness; to disbelieve is to lose this honor.

Compliments and careful listening like this will help one make friends easily, both in social situations and in the psychic market. Also note how vaguely defined the powers and abilities of this psychic truly were. First, the psychic claimed the ability to "read" what was going on in this person's life through seemingly telepathic means. Later she claimed the ability to detect and see the spirits of the dead. Finally, as a third power, she claimed the ability to predict the future of the woman's daughter's life. Now there may be things in this world that we don't understand. It is, I suppose, conceivable that there are individuals who may be able to do things that science cannot explain at this time. But, when faced with this astonishing array of claimed powers in one individual, it seems more likely that classical fortune-telling and cold reading techniques are being used rather than paranormal abilities.

There's a very practical reason why such people keep their claims vague—the importance of the "shift" in fraudulent fortune-telling. Imagine the following exchange:

Psychic: "I sense children."
Client: "Yes."
Psychic: "You have a small child or children, right?"
Client: "No."
Psychic: "Well, this feeling is so strong. I think children are in your future."

YOUR OWN PERSONAL
PSYCHIC
As Seen on TV

• TAROT
• NUMEROLOGY
• CLAIRVOYANT
• ASTROLOGY
• I-CHING, RUNES

Specializing in
Difficult LOVE
Questions!

1•800•
1•900•

3.99/MIN • NO CREDIT CARD NEEDED

Must be 18 years or older to call

You have just witnessed a well-done shift. The psychic began by implying that he had the ability to sense whether the client had children or not. When this approach failed, he suddenly shifted his claim of knowing the present to knowing the future. A good fortune-teller is quite talented at this.

In the above example, if the client were to reply that he could not have children due to sterility or other complications, the telepsychic might respond by claiming that he would spend time around children shortly. Or that maybe he will adopt. Or that maybe medical science will find a cure for his problem. If he were to reply that he hated children, then the psychic could claim that either this was the "energy" that she was feeling and claim a hit, or she might try a new tactic. [9]

One could attempt to change the opinion of the client and thus provide a self-fulfilling prophecy. If the client claims that he hates children, the telepsychic might reply that he, in fact, did not hate them as much as he thought he did and should reassess his true feelings toward children. Or perhaps the psychic might knowingly state that his feelings will change in the future. If the psychic keeps insisting that the client's feelings are incorrect, subconsciously different, or will soon change, then he can never be proven wrong.

In some cases, such self-fulfilling prophecies can be dangerous. For example, some psychics claim the ability to sense medical problems. Such statements are often based on generalities, depending on the client's age. A typical exchange might go like this:

Psychic: "You have a pain in your back."

Client: "No, I don't."

Psychic: "Then someday you will."

Often what happens is that believing clients become so worried, agitated, and sensitive to any problem relating to their backs (or whatever body part was mentioned) that ultimately they do decide that they have back problems. Or heart problems or headaches or whatever it is that the psychic insists they have. (This is, by they way, how psychologists and anthropologists believe that voodoo curses work. The witch doctor tells his victim, a voodoo believer, that he is now cursed and will suffer greatly. The victim becomes so concerned and worried that he makes himself sick and sometimes even dies.)

In other cases, the psychic will advise the patient to get the alleged problem checked immediately. If nothing's found, then he will advise the patient to monitor the potential problem and claim that his powers are responsible for the continued well-being of the patient. If the patient works with the psychic, then they, "together," can keep him healthy. (Isn't it nice to have such people to help with problems?)

Oh, one more thing that simply must be inserted in here somewhere. If you're running a psychic phone line, don't forget to periodically bill your clients twice or even more for the same phone calls. Frequent callers won't even notice. Others don't bother, are too embarrassed, or don't know how to challenge it, and you get paid extra in all these cases. Overbilling is an important part of the 900 charge-by-the-minute telephone line business. Don't forget to take advantage of it. After all, the entire business is immoral, so why not go all the way. If you're going to steal people's money, steal it! [10]

But back to the psychics themselves. What about other, true predictions? The fact is that sometimes these people do say things that come true. Let me give you an example. As a starving writer, I have worked a lot of strange jobs. Not too long ago, I was working as a night guard in a downtown hotel in one of the many dumpy little decaying cities that characterize upstate New York and the Rust Belt in general. I was paid to roust drunks and drug-dealing youth (a job I always did as politely as possible) and to keep the clerk company so that nobody would attempt to kidnap her. This clerk was a nice young woman from the inner city who happened to be a firm believer in the powers of telepsychics. (Yes, Virginia, such people do exist.) Astonished, I asked her why she believed.

"Simple," she replied. One had predicted that she would receive an unexpected offer of marriage, and such an event had happened. (A fairly safe prediction for many women in their late twenties.) Then, she informed me, the telepsychic had also told her that she would a) receive a better job offer, b) travel abroad in the next few years, c) find romance, and d) gain a lot of money. She told me that she was still waiting on the other four, but since the first one had come true, the rest would undoubtedly happen in time. As all of the predictions were for good things, she was cheerfully awaiting the rest. [11]

The moral is clear: predict often and predict outrageously. We will repeat this again and again throughout this book. If you get a mere one in five correct, then you may find yourself with a believer for life. Keep things vague and open-ended so that you can merely claim that the prediction will come true but it just hasn't happened

yet. When you deal with individuals, keep the predictions positive so that they will be emotionally compelled to believe. When you deal with international and current events, keep it big enough so that it will impress others on the off chance that you somehow do get lucky. When you do get something right, record it and announce it loudly to all who care to listen. In time, people will believe.

(Among some skeptics this process is known as "the Jean Dixon effect." Jean Dixon is widely reputed to have predicted the Kennedy assassination. In fact, what she predicted was that a Democrat, any Democrat, would win the 1960 election and that he would die in office, but not necessarily in his first term in office. Jean Dixon has also predicted such events as the resignation from office of Jimmy Carter in mid-term, the start of World War III in 1958, the death of Fidel Castro in 1966, and that the Russians would be the first nation to put a man on the moon. Oops, oops, and double oops! Remember, if one wishes to make it in the fake psychic game, then you must publicize all successes and move beyond the failures by making even more predictions as soon as possible.) [12]

If one wishes to truly embarrass believers in psychic predictions, a cheap and easy method is to purchase a few supermarket tabloids featuring such predictions around the New Year holiday and save them. Pull them out the following New Years and show them to your friends. Don't just note the false predictions; also point out how many key events of the year were completely missed. Now remember, many of these psychics have not only been making such disastrously wrong predictions year after year, but they also continue to make their living by making such grossly inaccurate predictions year after year. Go figure, huh?

If you can't wait a year for results, simply survey persons credited as being talented psychics, asking who will win the next presidential election. Chances are you will note no more consensus about future events as predicted by psychics than you will about future events predicted by the general public. So much for psychics!

There is no convincing evidence that fortune-tellers or telepsychics have special powers other than those of deception and establishing rapport, which the rest of us can develop with a little training. In fact—and again, I was quite surprised when I first learned this—there is no convincing, repeatable, verifiable, nonanecdotal, universally accepted, scientifically admissible evidence that psychic powers exist at all.

Save your money. Avoid psychics. Avoid telepsychics in particular. If you're feeling desperate, call a legitimate hot line and let them help you through the crisis. They're better trained than the telepsychics and a heck of a lot cheaper. (In fact they're free!) If that's what it takes to get you through the problem, then there's nothing wrong with it. If you're feeling lonely, go out and participate in activities. Play sports, join clubs, attend religious services, do volunteer work. Just stay away from fortune-tellers. If you absolutely must try some fortune-telling and cannot live without some sort of "mystical advice," keep in mind that you can buy (and keep forever to consult repeatedly) a deck of Tarot cards or a copy of the I Ching for less than the cost of a five-minute phone call to one of these 1-900-EAT-CASH lines. All in all, there's got to be something better to do with your telephone and your money.

ADDENDUM 2-1

THE BARNUM EFFECT AND
A UNIVERSAL "PSYCHIC" READING

The Universal Reading shown below is a generic reading used by stage magicians and others who wish to give the impression of having supernatural insight into a subject's personality. The "Barnum effect," named after P.T. Barnum, the circus showman, is a term used to describe the manner in which some individuals will fool themselves into believing that such universal statements are aimed specifically at them personally. It has been shown with both anecdotal and experimental evidence that such universal statements often produce this affect among those who fail to recognize the universal nature of the statements.

"You have a great need for other people to like you and admire you. You have a tendency to be critical of yourself. You have a great deal of unused capacity which you have not turned to your advantage. While you have some personality weaknesses, you are generally able to compensate for them. Disciplined and self-controlled outside, you tend to be worrisome and insecure inside. At times you have serious doubts about whether you have made the right decision or done the right thing. You prefer a certain amount of change and variety and become dissatisfied when hemmed in by restrictions and limitations. You pride yourself on being an independent thinker and do not accept others' statements without satisfactory proof. You have found it unwise to be too frank in revealing yourself to others. At times you are extroverted, affable, and sociable, while at other times you are introverted, wary, and reserved. Some of your aspirations tend to be pretty unrealistic. Security is one of your goals in life."

ADDENDUM 2-2

THE SUN's PSYCHIC PREDICTIONS FOR MID-1995

According the June 13, 1995, issue of *The Sun* (Vol. 13, No. 24), a popular supermarket tabloid, here were the psychic predictions for the second half of 1995. *The Sun* states that Jean-Claude Dernier is a top psychic. "His accuracy rate is so tremendous that *The Sun* enlisted his aid in zeroing in on America through the end of the year," writes the paper. What a perfect opportunity to test the theory that one can make a reputation as a psychic by predicting often and predicting outrageously. Being a little bit psychic myself, I predict that if any of these do take place as predicted then, Mr. Dernier and *The Sun* will remind us all of the fact without ever again mentioning the many misses. So, with no further ado:

- The month of July will "barely be under way when raging infernos race through the dry timberland of the Pacific Northwest. Dozens will die, and there will be millions of dollars in property damage."
- This will immediately be followed by a Bigfoot bursting out of the woods to drag a hapless hunter off to his death. The Bigfoot, says Dernier, will kill the man to "prove how wrong killing can be."
- On or about July 30, a lethal virus outbreak will erupt near the Center for Disease Control in Atlanta, Georgia. Although it will be contained quickly, hundreds will die agonizingly painful deaths.
- In August, a terrorist bomb will destroy an entire New York City subway train, killing hundreds.
- In early September in Oklahoma, men digging a water well will strike it rich as they accidentally uncover "the largest oil reserve pocket ever seen." This will boost the nation's economy to unseen heights.
- In autumn, in Los Angeles, the entertainer Madonna will be vis-

ited by the Virgin Mary herself. The singer will then abandon her current lifestyle and devote herself to working with the poor and needy.

- One week later, Julia Roberts, the film actress, will abandon her acting career and become a "good-will ambassador for the United Nations."
- In October, Miami will be hit by another hurricane that will cause damage as far south as the Florida Keys and as far north as West Palm Beach. This same storm will cause floods in New Orleans.
- In November, "a large California community will be poisoned by a madman who slips toxic chemicals into its drinking water supply." This deadly poison will kill large numbers of men, women, children, and animals.
- "As 1995 winds down," the Great Lakes will be buried under large amounts of snow.

So there you have it, *The Sun*'s predictions for what to you is the past. If they have occurred as stated, return this book to the publisher, ask for your money back, and instead learn everything you can about psychic phenomena. Otherwise, give thought to not only what was predicted incorrectly, but also to what key events of the second half of 1995 Mr. Dernier forgot to mention completely. Also, note the way in which relatively mundane predictions (e.g., a hurricane in Florida and snowstorms in the Great Lakes) were included to refer to later as "accurate predictions," while outrageous statements involving Bigfoots and visitations from the Virgin Mary were included to get enough attention to merit publication and a sales boost.

Think about it.

ADDENDUM 2-3

THE *NATIONAL ENQUIRER'S* PSYCHIC PREDICTIONS
FOR THE SECOND HALF OF 1995

By contrast, the *National Enquirer* took a different approach in its June 20, 1995, edition. Instead of using just one alleged psychic, it used 10. Naturally, the tabloid forgot to point out that the 10 had failed to reach any consensus, thus bringing the entire point of the psychic predictions into question. They were also much more vague with the dates than *The Sun*, simply promising that the events would happen "sometime" in the second half of 1995.

So with no further ado, John Monti, alleged predictor of the shooting of President Reagan, tells us that . . .

*   Michael Jordan will retire from basketball once again, try out for professional hockey instead, wash out, and then return to professional basketball! There is no word of what his high school guidance counselor will think of this frequent career changing.
*   Chelsea Clinton, child of the Clintons, will guest star on the *Frasier* sit-com as Frasier's long-lost daughter and do an outstanding job!
*   Oprah Winfrey's "long time beau," Stedman Graham, will win $100 million in the Illinois lottery, run off to Hollywood, leaving Oprah behind, and date a string of beauties. But finally he'll change his mind and return to Oprah! Monti fails to predict who, if anyone, outside of the *National Enquirer*'s readership, cares.
*   Garth Brooks, the country singer, will replace Tom Hanks in a sequel to the film *Forrest Gump*. The song he writes for the movie, "Life is Like a Bowl of Chocolates," will become a smash country hit!

Barbara Donchess, alleged predictress of the Mount St. Helen's volcanic eruption, tells us to look forward to . . .

- George Clooney, star of the television show "ER," will be saved from a house fire by his pet pig!
- Bruce Springsteen will star in a new network drama called "Bruce." He will play an auto mechanic!
- Peter Jennings will become the first TV journalist to broadcast from the space shuttle!
- The O.J. Simpson murder trial will be suspended for 10 days while the entire jury recovers from a case of food poisoning received from a catered meal!

Laura Steele, "the renowned psychic who energizes the *Enquirer*'s "Blue Dot" [13] says that . . .

- Queen Elizabeth will step down as Queen of England. Prince Charles will succeed her and announce that he, in turn, will step down when his son, Prince William, reaches the age of 21.
- A seventh grader will build a working time machine out of parts he scoured from a microwave oven and present the device at his school science fair. Steele neglects to inform us if he will win the fair for this, or what his mom will say when she sees the microwave, but she does state that scientists will be impressed.
- Willie Nelson will claim to have been abducted by an alien spaceship and then release an album of 12 songs that the aliens taught him.

Judy Hevenly, the alleged psychic who benefits the world by being co-charger of the "Blue Dot," states that . . .

- The ratings of Jay Leno's "Tonight Show" will soar when he brings back Ed McMahon as his cohost. Unfortunately for Jay, David Letterman will lure Ed away with a large contract and then use him as his own cohost.
- Tim Allen, star of the TV show "Home Improvement," will be badly injured on the set and forced to spend time in traction. Fortunately for all concerned, the show will be aired so that it includes the accident scene, and it will set a record for ratings.

- Scientists in Florida will invent a device that will harness lightning and store its energy.

Lou Wright, who allegedly predicted the big 1989 San Francisco earthquake, warns us that . . .

- Mary Tyler Moore and Dick Van Dyke will return to TV as costars in an updated version of their classic show from 30 years ago.
- Bill Cosby will become U.S. ambassador to South Africa.
- Michael Jackson and wife, Lisa Marie Presley, will star in a very successful remake of the classic motion picture *Casablanca*, taking on Humphrey Bogart's and Ingrid Bergman's parts, respectively.

Micki Dahne, alleged predictor of a fatal Canary Island jet explosion, tells us that . . .

- Dolly Parton's husband will launch his own singing career by releasing an album of duets with his wife.
- Baseball fans will go on strike, boycotting games during the last few weeks of next season.
- Scientists will discover a virus that will turn rocks into food. Some experts then predict that this will lead to an end to hunger.

Clarisa Bernhardt, alleged foreseer of Florida's Hurricane Andrew, predicts that . . .

- Demi Moore will trigger a riot by dancing topless in a public bar.
- John Goodman will team up with Richard Simmons to host a weight loss cruise in the Caribbean. Unfortunately, Goodman will jump ship after deciding that the regimen is not providing him with enough food.
- Animal rights activists will free the killer whale who starred in the motion picture *Free Willy* by hoisting him out of his cage and releasing him into the ocean.

Marie Graciette, yet another famous psychic, tells us that . . .

- Sally Jesse Raphael will quit TV, stating that she is tired of sleazy guests. (We can only hope . . .)
- Arnold Schwarzenneger will announce his plans to make a Tarzan movie alongside the original chimp, Cheetah, star of the 1930s movies. Cheetah is still alive and well and living in Florida.
- Jerry Seinfeld will retire from TV and become a world famous marine biologist who works to save endangered species.

Leah Lushner offers us such predictions as . . .

- Bruce Willis, action movie star, will foil a hijacking. The militant hijacker will allegedly wish to commandeer a plane to the Falkland Islands.
- A billionaire will start a new apocalyptic cult, and they will all move to an underwater city hundreds of miles off of the Atlantic coast.
- Pamela Anderson will almost leave the show "Baywatch." Her husband will patch things up by offering producer, David Hasselhoff, the opportunity to sing on one of his Motley Crue albums.

Finally, Shawn Robbins, who allegedly predicted the assassination attempt on the Pope, tells us all to be on the look out for . . .

- Hugh Hefner will retire, giving up his Playboy empire to become a sunflower farmer!
- Twelve members of Congress will refuse all of their pay until the budget is balanced! (Yeah, right.)
- Tonya Harding will be denied permission to open the nation's first all-nude ice skating rink!

ENDNOTES

1   James Randi is a magician, writer, and investigator of unusual phenomena and paranormal claims. He is also, from time to time, a troublemaker. Project Alpha was a controversial incident where he trained two men in ways to imitate psychic phenomena and then arranged to have them tested by a parapsychology laboratory. When they passed and were certified as being "truly psychic," he gleefully confessed the prank to all the world.

2   Actually, the person claimed to be a "shaman," not a psychic. Once, long before the allegations came to light, I actually had lunch with him. Although he was charismatic and told many enjoyable stories, he was unable to discuss shamanism knowledgeably in an anthropological sense.

3   See Marlock and Dowling's *License to Steal* for more details.

4   There are a variety of sources on reading body language. Some caution is in order, though, as many have a pseudoscientific aspect and feel to them (kind of like fortune-telling and psychic readings themselves). One videotape that has some use is Lee Lapin's *Expert Body Language: The Science of People Reading*, available from Paladin Press.

5   The science of studying the way language use relates to one's position in society is known as "sociolinguistics," and it can be a fascinating subject.

6   Saville and Dewey, *Red Hot Cold Reading*.

7   Keene's book is listed in the bibliography. The fact that he was shot comes from James Randi's *Flim-Flam*, p. 246.

8   Gordon, *Channeling into the New Age*, p. 73.

9   In one of my all-time favorite shifts that I saw on a paid psychic hot line infomercial, an incorrect claim about a romance was shifted from the present to a past lifetime during the U.S. Civil War! Oh, you gotta love it, even as you

hate it. The client seemed entertained, in any case. Of course, she could have seen a whole movie or bought a book for the cost of two minutes of the telepsychic's time.

10 For a really fine piece giving the inside scoop on the big business of telephone psychics, see "Telephone Psychics: Friends or Phonies," by C. Eugene Emery, Jr., in *Skeptical Inquirer*, Vol. 19, No. 5, Sept./Oct. 1995.

11 Let's assume that this hotel clerk makes $6 an hour, works 40 hours a week, and makes one 16-minute phone call to her "psychic advisor" at $3 a minute. That's $48, or the equivalent of eight hours, or one full day, of work, ignoring taxes. That's a sizable chunk of money to such a person.

12 These Jeane Dixon predictions come from Neher's *The Psychology of Transcendence*, p. 161-162. More Dixon mispredictions are recounted in Randi's *Flim-Flam*, p. 9, and Nickell and Baker's *Missing Pieces*, p. 155-157. Nickell and Baker cite Christopher's 1970 work, *ESP, Seers, and Psychics* as their source, but this book is out of print and very difficult to get ahold of.

13 The *National Enquirer* regularly features "The Lucky Blue Dot." This dot has allegedly been charged with psychic energy, and the *Enquirer* states that "just rubbing it could turn your life around." The June 20, 1995, issue of this fine publication includes articles praising the benefits of the dot. Headlines credit it with accomplishments such as:

> "The Blue Dot helped my tiny princess become
> a beauty queen."
> "My daughter cashed in on a TV game show."
> "I hit the jackpot for $50,000."
> "Bingo! The Blue Dot won me $30,000."

Mere Entertainers, or Cosmic Vanguards of a Psychic Master Race?

Telekinesis, and a Few Miscellaneous Tips on Creating a Reputation as a Psychic

"What!" cried the pilgrim. "'Tis nothing but base trickery!"
"Uhhh, I guess so. But it works for me," said Pete as he twisted open the cap on another cold bottle of beer. The top came off with an audible pop and a hiss of escaping gas.

"Your psychic reading is nothing at all! Hollow fluffery and pomp! Your prophecies for the future are vague at best, simply foolish at worst."
"Well, yeah, but then again, a lot of people do believe in these things. Besides, I even had you fooled for a while."

"Zounds," cried the pilgrim, angrily waving his solid staff in the air. "I have climbed all the way to the top of this mountain in search of the miraculous. I demand to see you work your powers!"

The guru

reached into the back pocket of his jeans as he slowly set the beer down on a nearby rock. "Okay, okay, just watch. Now you're really going to see something neat." The eerie scene was lit by nothing but the dim glare of the small television screen. Slowly he drew out his hand, revealing a badly mangled piece of silverware.

"See this spoon? I did this to it just yesterday using nothing but the powers of my mind. Didn't touch it at all. Honest," snickered the guru. "Shame you missed it."

"Aye, verily!" gasped the pilgrim in amazement. "Oh wise teacher, can you teach me how to accomplish such awesome feats of supernatural ability?"

"Hmmm, I don't know. My powers are kinda fickle, but we'll see what we can do."

The pilgrim leaned forward and the lesson began . . .

Among the most spectacular of all alleged psychic phenomena is "telekinesis," or the claimed ability to mysteriously affect material objects through the power of thought alone. This chapter will describe some of the methods by which you can falsify this phenomenon. Skeptics claim, and they have some convincing arguments, that these are the actual methods by which so-called "real psychics" have convinced millions of believers and some scientists that these powers exist.

First of all, like so many things surrounding the unexplained phenomenon, the most essential ingredient for being perceived as a purveyor of mysterious psychic forces is *reputation*. In the wild and wacky world of the paranormal, reputation is everything; reality is nothing. Do anything and everything you can to achieve a reputation for being able to command and control mysterious forces. When you have achieved this sort of reputation, eager fans will flock to you expecting miracles. If you give them something that even slightly resembles a miracle, then they will usually be quite impressed and tell all of their friends about the "amazing thing" that they saw. And it's generally quite safe to bet that as they exaggerate the story through repeated tellings, your reputation will grow even more.

In some cases, this goes double for the media. Have you ever noticed how all of the really famous reporters tend to spend a lot of time in war zones and disaster areas? I mean, some of these people will cheat, lie, steal, and stab each other in the back just for the opportunity to tromp around on film inside a horribly contaminated toxic waste spill site that's still glowing with deadly radiation. [1] There's a reason for this—it is easy to do a spectacular story on spectacular events.

Sometimes, when discussing a psychic phenomenon, the media exaggerates the incident in order to make the story more sensational and thus easier to write. Although this would normally be a serious violation of journalistic principles, paranormal claims are often lumped into the category of "fluff," equal in importance to trained dogs, barking fish, the local elementary school production of Little Red Riding Hood, or the misshapen carrots featured in "Ripley's Believe It or Not" cartoons. In fact, as mentioned in the last chapter, there's an entire genre of goofy pseudo documentaries that knowingly distort the facts surrounding such claims and then dismiss their lack of ethics as "entertainment." Unfortunately, with all the hype, naturally there are people who do take these things seriously. [2]

Even when there are sincere witnesses, the process of exaggeration frequently happens, sometimes unknowingly. This is helped along by the way the human memory works. Human memory, contrary to its reputation, is far from infallible. It frequently distorts and exaggerates events, particularly those that have had a strong emotional impact. The more time that goes by since the event, the more the happening gets twisted. Stage magicians have noticed that there is a tendency among their fans to "improve" descriptions of their own tricks. Many have remarked on the peculiarity of listening to fans excitedly praise them for having done tricks that they not only didn't do but are technically incapable of doing and would find far beyond their capabilities, if not the laws of physics. With psychics who "really" do "real" tricks, this phenomenon is even more pronounced. (Thus, once again, as described in the last chapter, scientists and the scientific establishment insist on maintaining a standard of acceptance for phenomena that is hinged on the *repeatability* and *verifiability* of a claimed effect.)

The easiest way to fake many psychic stunts is, in effect, to do a magic trick. Therefore, in order to understand the means of faking psychic powers, we must have some knowledge of how magic tricks work and are remembered.

The basic idea behind magic tricks, or "conjuring" as the magicians like to call them, is that you do one thing but make it look like something much more impressive. This is normally done through taking advantage of the human powers of observation and the magician's ability to "misdirect" these observations so that the viewer only notices what the magician wishes him to.

In the case of fraudulent psychics, both of these principles hold true. They may meet a scientist, a media person, or any individual and give them a "psychic demonstration." As the years go by, and the impressed witnesses repeat their account of what happened, those who weren't there will be left with a description of an event that they can in no way explain. Even a good magician with the ability to reproduce such an effect often cannot explain what happened accurately, as they weren't there, and the observers did not notice the details that a magician would look for. Furthermore, the event has now grown and been distorted.

But enough of this reality stuff! Let's get to the hoaxing. So with no further ado, we now jump into bending spoons. There is a great deal of evidence to suggest that this trick was used by "real psychics" in the past to fool physicists, reporters, and others.

SPOON BENDING

For some reason, spoon bending was all the rage about 20 years ago. This was due to some charismatic "psychic" entertainers who did the talk show circuit and put on performances of their powers. Why they chose spoon bending as their power we may never know, but the fact is that today, spoon bending, curiously, is seen as a psychic marvel.

There are several means by which spoons can be bent. The simplest one, which also happens to be the worst, is described fully in Addendum 3-1. That's it—the loser method to imitate psychic spoon bending. Easy, huh? Foolish too! I bet you are disappointed. I would be too. Nevertheless, there is evidence that this is exactly how some world-famous psychics established their reputations. [3]

There's a slight variation on this method where you bring a pre-bent spoon and switch it with one that is already present on the table. This one can be slightly more impressive, as it is possible to do some pretty bizarre things to a spoon in a home workshop. For example, you can take a vise and a well-padded pair of pliers and try putting a few corkscrew twists in the handle. That way nobody could possibly believe that you were simply using your fingers. Once again, for this trick to work well you must have somehow established beforehand a reputation as a psychic capable of bending spoons. Still, as the entire thing hinges on having the gall to do something obvious when nobody's looking, it's still pretty much a loser trick that would not impress any decent magician.

"What?" a reader might cry. "Is that it? I thought they held out the spoon at arms length and it drooped away right in front of them without

Illustration by Ted Kersten.

even being touched." Well, that is most certainly what the "psychics" would like you to think. Nevertheless, such an event has never been recorded on film. No one is able to do such an effect at will in front of a panel of scientists, especially when magicians are available to advise them on precautions to take to prevent sleight of hand from being used. In fact, it seems that this description has grown over the years as the story was repeated and exaggerated by believers and the media.

An interesting thing has happened, though. Over the years, magicians have found themselves pressed to explain and duplicate the spoon-bending effects of various alleged psychics, not as they necessarily happened but instead as people *thought* they happened. Therefore, magicians have come up with some truly impressive ways of bending spoons.

One of these, which you can use to impress those around you, is presented in Addendum 3-2. Practice it in front of a mirror. Develop the showmanship to pull it off. By the time you are done, you'll have a trick that you can do with pride.

As with all magic tricks, there are multiple means by which you can produce the same effect. For example, a Chinese gentleman by the name of Leung Ting states that it is possible to bend spoons in quite an impressive way by using special spoons made out of an easy-to-melt alloy known as Wood's metal. [4] Wood's metal can be melted either with very low temperatures, such as in a glass of tea, or with a slight dab of weak acid, such as common kitchen vinegar. [5]

To do this trick right, you actually need three spoons: one ordinary straight steel spoon, one pre-bent steel spoon, and a third spoon, identical to the others in form, style, and size, but made out of Wood's metal. (See Addendum 3-3 for the recipe for Wood's metal.) Showmanship comes into play when you convince your audience that the three spoons are one and the same. First, show them the straight steel spoon and allow them to inspect it at will. Then, using sleight of hand, switch it for the Wood's metal spoon. Do your stuff, wow them, impress them, and then if they wish to inspect what you have done, surreptitiously switch spoons again, handing them the pre-bent steel spoon.

As this requires a great deal of preparation to perform an effect that can be produced by easier means, I confess I haven't tried it yet. Nevertheless, it's presented here as an alternative method for use when people have almost figured out what you've been doing.

As if all of this were not enough, some of the larger mail order magic supply stores are offering commercially prepared gimmicked spoons that are designed to produce bending effects.

BENDING KEYS

Another foolish trick is bending keys. Once again, there are several means by which this can be done.

To produce a bend in a key, you can:

- Hold on really tight to the key at each end and bend with your fingers. Strength is needed here, particularly if you have a strong key.
- Put one end into something strong, metal, has a hole, and is reasonably secure. Push against the object and use leverage to help you produce the bend. Some easily available, innocuous objects that can be utilized for this purpose include some styles of belt buckles and the large openings where the key chain goes through on the ends of some styles of keys.
- Hold one end of the key firmly and then push it against a solid object or surface. A chair, the wall, or even the floor or part of a table can be utilized for this purpose. One good way to do this is to push down on a chair with one end of a key while you stand up and get out of the chair. This provides a lot of force on the key while keeping the force camouflaged as an ordinary movement.
- Place one key on top of the other and then push down on it. This works best with really long keys.

49

• Prepare a ring of pre-
bent standard keys.
Then switch a bent
key for a non-bent key.
Besides the obvious dis-
advantage of needing to
carry around a chain of
useless bent keys, the
bent key might not be
an exact duplicate of
the first one. The advan-
tage to it is that if you'd like you
can then "straighten" the key simply
by switching them back.

Bending keys is easy. Anyone can do it, and few people are
impressed by it in itself. If they were we would all be famous. The
trick comes in making people believe that the key has been bent
through out-of-the-ordinary means. A variety of ways to do this are
presented in Addendum 3-4. Once again, the factors needed to make
this work are showmanship, timing, and misdirection. Do not simply
hold up the key and announce that it's bent.

MOVING COMPASS NEEDLES

Many psychics have demonstrated the ability to move compass
needles. In some circles, this phenomenon has led to the theorization
by some intelligent people that telekinetic effects are electromagnet-
ic in nature. This conclusion is highly questionable. Because there
are several means by which such effects can be hoaxed, it would
probably have been much more appropriate if this observation had
led to increased precautions to prevent cheating.

Compass needles can be moved easily with a magnet. The trick
lies in finding a way to place the magnet next to the compass without being spotted. Avoid the obvious places, such as rings, necklaces,

and jewelry. Instead, attach a magnet under a shirt collar or next to your knee or elbow inside your clothing. You can even place one inside your mouth as long as you make sure it's clean and can find a way to do it so that you can still speak, eat, and do whatever you have to. The key to doing this successfully is to misdirect attention away from the magnet. Sometimes, ironically, it is easier to do this with two magnets instead of just one.

FIXING WATCHES AND CLOCKS

Starting and stopping watches is a frequent part of psychic demonstrations. If done with an emphasis on showmanship and the proper exuberance and "energy," the effect can be startling. Once again, there are several ways to do this, most of them relatively simple.

- Often a stuck watch can be restarted simply by rewinding it and then giving it a shake. Of course, you can't just do this and then hand people the watch. You must do it while appearing to do something mystical, and then hand them the "healed" watch.
- A large number of watches become stuck and won't work properly when their inner workings become jammed with dust and gummy oil. Frequently, if you take such a watch and handle it for a few minutes, then your body heat alone will be enough to heat up the old oil and get the watch working again.

On one occasion, a pair of psychologists became curious as to whether this method would work to explain how a once prominent psychic could seem to restart stopped watches easily and frequently. They recruited seven local jewelers to try this method and then measured their rate of success. It was found that out of the 106 watches attempted, 60 of them (or 57 percent) were started using this method. [6] Of course, you must stall for a few minutes while waiting for the watch to start, but a good showman can easily find something to do. You could look at the watch and shout, "Run! Run!" or you could regale your audience with stories about how difficult life has been growing up with these awesome powers of yours. Or perhaps this would be a good opportunity to remind the audience how your powers only perform erratically and thus you cannot guarantee results (thus showing your "sincerity," as they presume a true trickster would be able to perform 100 percent of the time).

- Plant confederates who will hand you working watches for you to fix. Say, "Oh my, a broken watch." Then start it. If you can't make this look good, give up, as you will never be able to make it as a fraudulent psychic.
- If you should ever establish enough of a reputation to get yourself booked on a talk show, then you can occasionally show up with a small working watch that has no second hand and operates silently. Without close inspection or a good look at the minute hand on two separate occasions, it is virtually impossible to determine if such a watch is working or not. (And naturally you won't give the TV or radio audience the opportunity to do this!) Even if the host determines that this is what you have done, it is unlikely he will blurt it out on the air. To do so would be rude and make his show less spectacular.
- Use a gimmicked clock or watch. There are several ways to do this. Some involve squeezing the plastic face plate at a given point so that the second hand can't run beyond it. Others involve switching or pushing a button on the back of the clock. By the way, if you would like to really impress people, one way is to collect a large number of broken clocks and watches together. When you get ready to demonstrate your powers, make sure that you have a couple of gimmicked versions in the pile. If you can surreptitiously

insert a watch that runs either backward or outrageously fast, then the effect will be impressive.

- If you ever get the opportunity, a great variation of this can be performed on a radio call-in talk show. First instruct members of the audience to find a broken watch from somewhere around their house or apartment. A sizable number of listeners will do so. At some point during the show, inform the audience that they should hold their broken watches in their hands and focus their energies on getting their watches to work. You will use your powers to assist them. Naturally, the heat of their hands will make a sizable portion of these watches work. Not all, of course, but a large number. After a few minutes, encourage those who had their watches start to call in and give testimonials. A large number of people will do so. You can then take the credit for it all.

MAKING A WATCH SPEED UP

This is another trick that is occasionally demonstrated by self-proclaimed psychics. The effect is as follows: the psychic takes a watch from an audience member. He examines the watch, compares the time it shows to the time on his own watch, and then hands it back to the owner, placing it in their palm. They close their hand firmly around the watch, gripping it tightly. The psychic then concentrates, gesticulates, self-flagellates, expectorates, and does whatever else he feels a psychic should do in order to look authentic. Finally, he announces that he is through and instructs the mark to now examine the watch. Wow! Is it a time warp? Is it some kind of weird "quantum physics" effect? [7]

As with most psychic phenomena, the actual happenings are not that incredible. What happens is that at some point the psychic twists the knob on the watch, turning the hands a few hours ahead. The exact time that the watch is forwarded to is completely unimportant.

He then hands the watch to the mark and places it face down in his palm. If he'd like, he may instruct him to place his finger on the back of the watch and perhaps instruct him to use his "energy" to assist him by "focusing it and concentrating on the watch."

As with many tricks, the basic idea is simple but execution is difficult. Distraction and misdirection are important. In the excellent Nova video, *James Randi: Secrets of the Psychics*, Randi demonstrates this, among other "psychic" marvels, to a class of college freshmen. If one watches carefully, you can see how he distracts the audience by asking a student to put out her hand. When she does, he smiles and says, "No, the clean hand." He then begins playfully laughing and joking with the woman about how he almost made her switch. A careful observer can notice that during the period when this give and take is happening, Randi is spinning the knob on the watch with his left hand. As most people's attention, naturally, is focused on Randi and the watch owner, this is not noticed easily. Of course, other methods of distraction and misdirection can and should be developed, but this is one useful example.

INVISIBLE THREAD TRICKS

If you wish to produce telekinetic effects, a nifty little product that you should be aware of is "invisible thread." Invisible thread is one of those spiffy toys, like Leggos or plastic vomit, that has a thousand and one uses, with the full variety being limited only by your imagination. Available at most magic supply shops for a surprisingly reasonable price, invisible thread looks like black thread that is beginning to fray. This is as it's supposed to be. To utilize the thread, you place it on a white surface and then ply off one, two, or three strands, depending on how much strength you wish your thread to have. It is recommended that you place a piece of tape or magician's wax on the ends of the thread that you wish to use so you will not lose it. [8] (After all, invisible thread is difficult to see.)

You can secretly attach this invisible thread to a variety of places on your hands or body. Some good places are buttons, particularly on one's wrist, or you can tie it to a ring on your finger. Once this is done, then you can use the invisible thread to either pull, push, or, from underneath, roll an item across a table. When your finished performing your stunt, then you can like simply roll up the thread or else surreptitiously break off the strand and place it on the floor.

BLOWING ON THINGS

In telekinesis the perceived effect is that something moves with no visible signs of being pushed. One simple way to provide an invisible push is to blow on something. Of course, you must blow surreptitiously, and naturally it helps to provide misdirection by waving your hands over the object as it moves (thus giving the impression that the object moves because your hands pass over it rather than through some more mundane cause).

I know of two different occasions when this technique was used to imitate psychic phenomena. The first involved the rolling of pencils across tabletops through gently blowing on them, with the hand kept over them as they rolled to simulate a mysterious force emanating from the hand. The second involved opening a phone book and turning the pages by blowing. In this case, too, the effect was enhanced through meaningful-seeming gestures and expressions.

MATERIALIZING OBJECTS

When it comes time to materializing other people's belongings, you are really on very shady ethical ground. But then again . . . who cares! If you are going to be a fraudulent psychic, you might as well go all the way, right? Take the suckers for all they're worth!

The effect (and perceived phenomenon) is that you somehow supernaturally use your superhuman psychic powers to recover and "materialize" someone else's missing property, something valuable and dearly loved that the believer has missed for a considerable period of time. Finally, after having searched high and low, they come to you and your awesome powers in desperation. After much mumbo-jumbo and a lot of presto-chango, you, lo and behold, materialize the item from nowhere!

How do you do this? Well, its highly complex, but we're going to teach you anyway. The process is described in Addendum 3-5 in complete detail.

PLAYING GAMES IN THE LABORATORY
AND OTHER ONE-SHOT METHODS
TO AMAZE SCIENTISTS AND THE GENERAL PUBLIC

As we've mentioned time and time again, telekinetic powers defy the laws of physics. If this is the case, then why should yours be limited to a certain set of practiced routines? Instead, if you see the chance to fool somebody and mislead them into thinking that you possess the ability to do the miraculous, then go for it! If you are in already, why not take the total plunge. Few people ever became famous by being half-hearted.

Remember, what you are doing essentially is committing a hit-and-run guerrilla warfare campaign with other people's notions of reality. You are playing mean and cruel games with their heads. Get them when they're not expecting it! The believers will love you for it and swear that you and your powers are real even as you steal their money and take advantage of them. When the skeptics come along and write a book like this, giving out the secrets of your techniques, don't worry. Some poor sucker who trusts you will look them right in the eye and say, "All right, so you've explained the spoon bending and the materialization, but what about the time he _____ ? Until you explain that, then I'm going to keep right on believing in him and his superhuman, awesome, amazing powers."

When this happens, then be sure to thank the true believers sincerely. Look them in the eye. Shake their hand. Tell them that the world needs more open-minded, positive people such as themselves. Then steal their money! Why not? You are a crook after all, and such is your nature, so people with half a brain should expect it.

The following will serve as pointers.

• There was one famous psychic who used a pair of confederates to enter restaurants and other public places where the psychic was scheduled to be interviewed shortly before the session was scheduled to take place. The confederates would use their imaginations and ingenuity to create dozens of minor and peculiar incongruities. For example, they would secretly turn the clocks on the wall a few hours ahead or back. They would go to empty tables close to where the interviewer was likely to sit and then bend the silverware in odd ways. Pictures would be tilted on the walls.

You can employ people to do the same thing. As the interview progresses, the restaurant staff and patrons will begin to notice the results and do things such as adjust the clocks to their proper times and request that the waiter bring them functional silverware. The interviewer will inevitably notice at least some of these peculiar events and comment on them. When this happens, look them straight in the eye and say something such as, "You know, isn't that strange? These things happen around me all the time, and I can't even explain it myself!" They may put it in their interview.

• Although it doesn't really count as telekinesis, instead falling more under the category of prediction and precognition, you can do a great deal to boost your reputation as a psychic by following current events. When something really earth shattering should occur, such as an assault on the president, a spectacular plane crash, or a prominent natural disaster, have a friend call the media and tell them something like, "You know, isn't it incredible? Just last week my friend Pete the psychic told me that this was going to happen just like it did." With some luck, they might just print it, in which case you show this "proof" of your powers to anyone you can get to look at it. If not, they will simply dismiss your friend's claim as a crank call, and you will have lost nothing.

- Whenever you have the chance to be tested, accept it. If you see a chance to cheat, take it. For example, there are many, many ways that psychics have passed laboratory testing through cheating and thereby passed inspection and improved their reputation. Many of these are not in this book for space reasons and also because many of these techniques would only work well under the conditions where the psychic used them. For example, there is one famous psychic who passed a laboratory test where he "clairvoyantly" viewed the results of dice rolling in a shut box. It has been pointed out that the scientist involved was very nearsighted and that the psychic was allowed to handle the box after every test and could clearly have had opportunity to peak inside. If he had, the nearsighted scientist would have been unlikely to have caught him. Although no one can prove that this is what happened during the experiment, it is undoubtedly significant that the psychic in question has refused to be tested again under conditions that would be better controlled.

- Similarly, utilize any photos taken during the test to your advantage. While living in Taiwan, I decided to visit a self-proclaimed "chi kung master" who had promised, over the telephone, to show his powers to me. Instead, he embarked on a rambling dialogue about how he had these truly incredible powers and would like to demonstrate them today but just couldn't, as it would use too much power and blah, blah, yackety yack, and on and on he went for half an hour, managing to completely contradict himself more than half a dozen times on several key points, until there was absolutely no doubt in my mind that the man was a total charlatan, made famous through nothing but his extensive advertising in Taiwan's English-speaking newspapers.

He did, however, show me his scrapbooks. Included among the many photos were some that he proudly told me showed him as the subject of a scientific experiment. Unfortunately, the experiment was badly flawed in several places. First of all, an electrical engineer was shown testing the brain waves of the chi kung master while he utilized telekinesis (or the chi kung equivalent). When I asked why brain waves were being tested by an electrical engineer, he told me that it was because brain waves were electrical in nature. This is essentially true, but if followed to its logical extreme, it would mean that you should take a broken toaster to a psychiatrist. The most serious flaw in the "experiment," however, was that nothing was being done to see if the man actually had telekinetic powers—it was already assumed to be the case. In fact, the object to be moved was hung from the ceiling in such a way that *the tester had his back turned to it!* He could not see the man or his assistant while looking at his brain wave monitor. They were completely unobserved and could easily push, blow, or by other physical means cause the object to swing as promised!

Although the experiment is obscure, the test subject used many photos from it as "proof" of his powers and as publicity for his chi kung school, to which he would lure wealthy students to sign up for lots of expensive classes in how to do many unlikely things.

- At another laboratory, there is evidence that there were holes in the walls left over from some reworked wiring. Critics have pointed out that the results of an experiment in "clairvoyantly transmitting pictures" can be partially explained by the possibility of a confederate (who was definitely present) passing pictures through the holes in the walls. An excellent idea, if you should ever find yourself in a parapsychology laboratory undergoing electrical work with your confederate on the other side of the wall with holes in it!

- If you're really disgusting, then you can do as one prominent psychic did. If a journalist who has criticized you should suffer serious misfortune or die suddenly, say something publicly such as, "Oh my! That's terrible! I hope I'm not responsible. It always makes me so upset when these things happen to my critics, and I always feel so terrible afterwards. I do so wish that I could control my powers better."

- Don't restrain your confederates. Encourage them to use their imaginations too. For example, one time a psychic was being interviewed by a journalist in a public tram car. His confederate, who was unknown to the journalist and standing outside of his view, pulled the emergency brake, bringing the tram car to a sudden, screeching halt. The psychic apologized for "unconsciously doing that" and "not having better control of my powers." The journalist was quite impressed and included the incident prominently in his story. (Don't let those confederates become too well known to the media, though, or this sort of thing just won't work well.)

And remember, one of the great things about fraudulent psychic powers is that, unlike real phenomena, they know no limits. If you can imagine it, then fake it, then claim it, somebody somewhere is likely to believe you, and if they are a journalist or a celebrity, then your career as a psychic is established for some time. Once you have a reputation, thousands or even millions will believe in you and your nonexistent powers. Then, after they trust and believe in you, you can steal their money. After all, that's what the fraudulent psychic game is all about!

ADDENDUM 3-1

PSYCHIC SPOON BENDING—THE LOSER METHOD

STEP ONE—Get a reputation for having psychic powers. (This is normally done by lying to large numbers of people, including gullible friends and media representatives.)

STEP TWO—Tell people that your powers include the ability to bend spoons using your mind power.

STEP THREE—Invite a number of fans (and media representatives, of course) to see a demonstration of your superhuman spoon-bending abilities.

STEP FOUR—Promise them that you are going to bend a spoon for them using your incredible psychic spoon-bending abilities.

STEP FIVE—Promise them again that you are going to bend a spoon for them with your amazing, psychic spoon-bending abilities.

STEP SIX—Promise them again that you are going to bend a spoon for them using your unearthly, psychic spoon-bending abilities.

STEP SEVEN—Promise them one more time that you are going to bend a spoon using your awe-inspiring, psychic spoon-bending abilities.

STEP EIGHT—When none of these people are paying attention (their attention spans should have worn pretty thin by now), bend the spoon using your fingers or by pushing on the table or some equally simple and stupid method.

STEP NINE—Yell, "Gosh! Wow! You people just missed seeing me bend a spoon with my superhuman, incredible, amazing, unearthly awe-inspiring abilities! And just when you were all looking away! I am so sorry that I can't control these superhuman, amazing, unearthly awe-inspiring psychic abilities so that you all could have a better look at what you just missed!"

STEP TEN—Remind the people who were present again and again about how they saw you bend the spoon. A sizable percentage of them will be too embarrassed to admit that they were looking the wrong way when this incredible event happened and they will nod their heads and agree with you. Some will even announce that they saw it and were there.

STEP ELEVEN—Tell the world that you bent a spoon in front of a room full of witnesses. Remind them all again and again of how you can do this. Use your imagination. Glue bent spoons all over your car or do something equally foolish. At every chance you get, work to establish a reputation as a psychic spoon bender. Remember the Golden Rule of being a fraudulent psychic: "Once you have established a reputation so that others will believe that you are truly psychic, your believing fans will do the rest."

As the loser method relies on producing the bend while nobody is looking, the psychic can be helped by producing large amounts of chaos during a spoon-bending session (or "experiment" if you are that egotistical). If people are paying too much attention as you stare at the spoon doing nothing, then you may get up and run around for a while. Screech loudly that sometimes, for some inexplicable reason, your powers work best when the spoon is in close proximity to metal and/or running water. As you run around looking for water and metal, you may have an opportunity to surreptitiously bend the spoon.

ADDENDUM 3-2

SPOON BENDING—THE FINESSE METHOD

The basis of the finesse method of spoon bending, like all good magic tricks, is showmanship. Showmanship is one of those things that can't easily be learned from a book. [9] For example, a friend of mine is charismatic and outgoing and enjoys gathering a group of people together as he does this. He promises to show them a psychic miracle and then begins to work the crowd. In order for this to work, he says, they all must focus their energy and believe, truly believe, that he can bend the spoon. Then he goes to work with the trick.

Myself, I'm more laid back and quiet. Instead, I simply sit there and say how some people can bend spoons and isn't that amazing and I wonder just how they could do that anyway? And then, lo and behold, much to everyone's surprise, including, apparently, my own, the spoon bends!

Like many tricks, this one depends on a prepared and slightly gimmicked object. Fortunately, you can easily make this yourself. First, get an ordinary stainless steel spoon. Don't use silver spoons for this because 1) they don't bend right, and 2) this trick wrecks the spoon, and silver costs too much to do this for a simple trick.

Prepare the spoon by carefully bending the stem back and forth time and time again. Ultimately, the metal will begin to develop a hairline fracture where you are bending it. Stop before it breaks, but make sure that it is close to breaking. In order to hide this process, as, of course, you should, you may either do this where nobody can see, such as under the table while your companions are eating, or else do it in advance and hide the spoon in your pocket so that nobody can see that you are carrying a spoon around with you. Later, you can switch it with a proper, ungimmicked spoon.

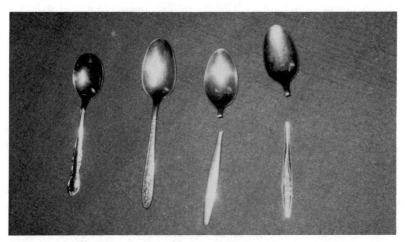

Before you can "bend" a spoon, you need to create a hairline crack in it. Be sure the spoon doesn't crack in half before you are ready for it to do so.

with the crack on the handle and hold it up. Make sure that you hold it with your thumb and finger covering the crack. Say what you're going to say in order to get everyone's attention and then begin to slowly, ever so slowly, stroke the spoon. You must be gentle. The entire idea is that the audience must believe that there is no way that you could possibly be bending the spoon using your strength. Instead, those watching must firmly believe that there is something at work here that they do not and probably cannot fathom. Something mystical. And since you are only using a very gentle motion, there is no way that you could be bending an ordinary spoon using just the amount of pressure you are using. What they don't know, of course, is that the spoon is weakened so that the amount of pressure needed to bend it is reduced.

Ultimately the spoon will bend. Some people at this point will ask the audience to assist them with the stroking so that they can see and feel for themselves that the spoon is bending with just a very slight pressure. Finally, if you continue long enough, and there's no reason why you shouldn't, the spoon will break right in half.

As with many magic tricks, the basic idea is simple. The skill comes in executing and performing it in an impressive way.

ADDENDUM 3-3

WOOD'S METAL

Wood's metal is a metal alloy with an extremely low melting point. It can be made by combining the following metals:

50% Bismuth
25% Lead
12.5% Tin
12.5% Cadmium

The metals can be powdered and then melted in a copper container.

ADDENDUM 3-4

SOME COMMON METHODS OF SHOWING A BENT KEY SO THAT IT APPEARS TO BE STRAIGHT

As stated in the text, bending a key without getting caught is relatively easy. The trick lies in presenting a bent key to a viewer so that it appears to be bending as they watch. The following are two methods by which this can be done. Both involve sleight of hand and require practice before they can be done well.

1) Hold a pre-bent key so that you cover the bend with your left hand and only present the straight portion. Sometimes it helps to place the key down on a table top so that the flat part lies along the plane of the table.

2) With your left hand still holding the key in such a way that the bend is concealed, begin stroking the remaining straight part of the key. As you stroke the key, begin slowly revealing the bend just a little at a time in such a way that it appears to increase every few strokes. When the bending is done, then you may simply hand the mark the key.

This process can be done in at least a couple different ways. The first is to hold the bent end of the key between your thumb and forefinger as shown in the illustration. As you do the trick, simply slide your thumb back little by little. This movement should be as discreet and hidden as possible, but it may help to conceal some of it anyway with your right hand.

A second way is to place the key on the table with the flat end projecting and resting on the table top. The bent end is held, concealed, in the left hand. If you'd like you may even request that the mark place a fingertip on the projecting end of the key. If you do this, you may speak of how it often gets warmer as you stroke the key. Make sure while stroking that you ask him if he can feel it getting warmer. If nothing else, then a brief discussion along the lines of "isn't it strange that he doesn't feel it get warmer while so many others do" will distract him from the matter at hand. Then, as you stroke, gently continue to press down on the key, making it appear to bend in front of you.

ADDENDUM 3-5

MATERIALIZATION

In order to "materialize" a missing object, the following sequence of steps should be followed.

1) Find someone. Get them to trust you. Then lie to them a lot. Tell them you have psychic powers. Do whatever it takes to make them believe in you and your nonexistent powers.
2) After they trust you and believe that you have psychic powers, then steal something of theirs. Ideally, it should be something that they value and will miss greatly once it's gone. Heirlooms and mementos are perfect for this sort of thing.
3) Don't work too quickly here. Make sure, that they really miss something before you decide to materialize it.
4) Let them come to you, hoping, in desperation, that you can somehow use your awesome powers to recover the object.
5) Then go through some mumbo-jumbo nonsense. Make it as dramatic as possible. Remember, it doesn't need to be overly sensible, just dramatic.
6) When they are not looking (distract them if you have to), pull out the object and place it on the table. Don't damage it. This detracts from the procedure.
7) When they notice that the object is now on the table, act amazed. Tell them that you don't understand exactly how this happens yourself, but that somehow these things occur all the time around you. State that you are glad that you could use your superhuman powers for good in order to help a dear person like them to recover their missing object.

8) Carefully remember their name. If you need money later, ask them for a donation. Tell them you are being persecuted or something. Tell them you need the money to engage in research to help the world understand your miraculous powers. Heck, tell them anything. Just get the damn money and put it in your bank account and spend it before someone catches on to what you're really doing!

The following variations might prove helpful. If you really want to create an illusion that is inexplicable, find a friend or make the acquaintance of someone who is as slimy as you are and is also involved in the fake psychic routine. Then have him steal things for you from believers in one place, and you steal things for him from believers in another part of the country. Little old widows are ideal for this. Then swap the stolen goods and show up in the area where your accomplice stole the stuff. Just think how amazed the believers will be when you, having met them for the first time, suddenly materialize the long missing watch of their dearly departed, greatly missed husband George! Oh what a clever and funny trick! But don't forget to ask them for a donation afterward. After all, that is the point of the thing.

Another option is if a believer, especially a believer with many small children, should take you for a ride in the family car, don't forget to grope around under the seat when they are paying attention to steering through traffic. Although you risk getting something sticky and gross all over your fingers, you might just find something really neat, like a small child's toy or perhaps, on rare occasions, a piece of jewelry of some sort. Take it home, dust it off some, and then materialize it at a later date, much to everyone's amazement.

Similarly, when friends, media personalities, and especially believers invite you to their homes and apartments, don't hesitate to secretively grope around behind the sofa cushions and other hard-to-reach places where lost valuables are likely to have been dropped or mislaid. If you find them, don't return them like a normal decent person would do. Instead, save them and materialize them later.

ENDNOTES

1   If you ever get a chance, you may ask my friend Daniel Nardini about this. Daniel, through no desire of his own, was the last American tourist to leave Beijing during the Tiananmen Square massacre. When the massacre broke out, he happened to be in Beijing and, for completely nonpolitical reasons, was visiting someone in some place where he was not supposed to be. Suddenly, the army gunned down the students and began rounding up everyone who, for whatever reason, happened to be in the wrong place during this very wrong time. Finally, after spending about a week or so hiding in a basement or closet on the wrong side of town, Daniel decided that it was now safe to come out, as the soldiers with the tanks and the AK-47s had calmed down a bit. When, much to everyone's amazement, he finally showed up at the American embassy, a group of reporters flocked around him, eagerly wishing to take him back out into the city with the sincere hope that he could show them something really terrible, emotionally disturbing, or, at the very least, dangerous. Apparently, most of them had just flown in from Lebanon just to see the Tiananmen Square massacre, but they still weren't satisfied.

2   Perhaps this tendency to take flaky newspaper reports seriously reached its peak with the writings of Charles Fort (1874–1932), who wrote four book-length diatribes accusing the "scientific establishment" of ignoring any and all phenomena that did not fit in with their preconceived theories. Although much of Fort's material and commentaries are humorous and quite interesting, any serious impact that they might have had is blunted by his exclusive use of unverified newspaper reports as the source of his anomalies and his deadpan assumption that if it's in the paper it must be true.

3   For examples, you might read *The Psychology of the Psychic* by David Marks and Richard Kammann, *The Truth about Uri Geller* by James Randi, or *How to Play with your Food* by Penn and Teller.

4   Leung Ting has written a number of books on the martial arts and other aspects of Chinese culture. His two works on how fraudulent chi kung masters and

Chinese psychics operate are both listed in the bibliography. This trick comes from *Beyond the Incredibles*, pp. 136 and 156–157.

5   You could carry in your pocket a small cotton ball soaked in vinegar inside a matchbox or similar container. Dab your finger in the cotton and then dab it again onto the stem of the spoon where you wish to produce the melting effect.

6   Marks and Kammann, pp. 106–108.

7   Quantum physics is really, really weird, confusing, and counterintuitive. Many people like to make vague references to "quantum physics" because they feel it makes them sound smart and adds a scientific flavor to whatever idea they might currently be espousing. Such people almost invariably know nothing about quantum physics and would generally have a great deal of difficulty wading through a good, solid article on the subject in *Scientific American* magazine. For the record, although quantum physics is fascinatingly strange and well worthy of study, its practical effects on anything above the subatomic level range from negligible to nonexistent.

8   Magician's wax comes in a little cup and is used for a variety of purposes. In form it looks a little bit like a mixture of beeswax and snot. It is designed to be sticky and allow threads and other items to be stuck to various surfaces. Like invisible thread, it has a thousand and one uses.

9   For a good start, though, you might try *Magic and Showmanship* by Henning Nelms.

Can You Hear Me? Can You See Me?

Hoaxing Telepathy and Clairvoyance

"Surely you cannot be this cynical?"

"Whatta ya mean?"

"You have ignored the many unexplained miracles that abound throughout the world. 'Tis a terrible mistake."

"Whatta ya mean?"

"I mean, you base cur, that you have not even touched upon the miracles of mind reading and second sight. How does one explain such feats as these, oh most snotty one? Explain that, if you will."

"Uhhhh. Well. Okay . . ."

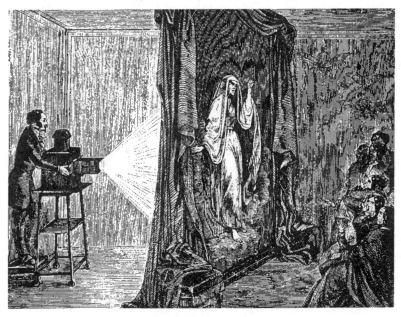

Among two of the most oft-claimed parapsychological phenomena are telepathy and clairvoyance. Telepathy is the alleged power of the mind to transmit thoughts to another person (or sometimes an animal) through special abilities lying outside of the normal means of communication. Clairvoyance is the alleged power of the mind to be able to see images of things that lie far outside of a person's normal realm of vision. [1] There has been a great deal of research into these subjects over the years. Some feel that this research has proven, through statistical analysis of many experiments, that such powers are real and do exist. Others feel that these experiments and the statistics kept on them were flawed through a variety of means and therefore prove nothing.

Martin Gardner, in his work, *How Not to Test a Psychic*, has shown how even slight opportunities for cheating can result in skewed test samples, with results "lying far beyond what can be explained by statistics and probability" if the test subject should choose to take advantage of these opportunities. For example, if a test subject should cheat successfully on only one out of six tests and not be caught, then this still gives results that cannot be explained by normal means by those who analyze the record of the test results. Such a situation, with slight but statistically significant deviations from chance, might occur if a test subject were, for example, to mark just one card in a sample of ten and then "guess" that one marked card correctly time and time again throughout a series of experiments.

Another possible flaw in many experiments is that if a test subject (usually a college student) shows evidence of success in telepathic abilities, then he or she is tested more often. Since test subjects are frequently rewarded for being part of the study, often with money or extra credit in a course they are taking, there is a clear motive for cheating. Thus, in many experiments if some subjects have been cheating successfully without being caught, then they will come back and be tested more often. Ultimately, any successful cheaters present will take part in a higher and higher percentage of the experiments conducted. This will end up with results that lie outside the normal realm of being statistically explicable.

It is for these reasons, among others, that most scientists are hesitant to accept many test results for psychic abilities if they cannot replicate the results in tightly controlled experiments of their own.

HOAXING TELEPATHY

Many of the methods by which such phenomena can be imitated or hoaxed are borrowed from "mentalism," the branch of conjuring and stage magic that demonstrates mental powers. Seeing things while blindfolded and performances featuring one participant "sending" thoughts to another are common mentalist acts.

Imagine the following dramatic scene in a large classical amphitheater sometime around the turn of the century. A tuxedoed performer with his mustache immaculately waxed stands on stage blindfolded quite securely. His assistant requests an item from the crowd. An eager fan offers the loan of an item, for example, a watch. The assistant then innocuously requests that the performer identify said item. The audience waits with anticipation to see if this is possible. Suddenly, after a dramatic pause, the performer states clearly and confidently, "It is a watch." Gasps of awe and hushed whispers ripple through the theater. The assistant returns the watch and requests another item from the fascinated crowd.

Today, in our post-television, high-speed world, such telepathic displays don't do as well as they used to. A performance of the type above could easily be recreated using a hidden microphone and small radio transmitter. Even if this method is not used, today's audience would find the performance simplistic and dull. Many such performers are at a loss of what to do. Some, such as the incomparable Penn and Teller, simply give a traditional magic show and spice up the performance with gallons of fake blood, bizarre gags, and menacing power tools. Most are content to eke out a living doing the same sort of performance, but to smaller, less demanding audiences. A few cheat, attempting to pass themselves off as real psychics by doing small, select performances to groups of egotistical scientists who believe themselves to be of such high intelligence that they will automatically catch the tricks by which mentalists fooled the audiences of the world years ago. Although the scientists might take precautions against the presence of radio transmitters, they will rarely be skilled enough to know how to prevent mentalist tricks. [2]

Codes

So, enough of these other people. How can you get in on the action and make a fast buck while making people think you've got super telepathic powers? The oldest technique for this is to use an innocuous code (such as the one shown in Addendum 4-1) in such a way that the audience will not suspect it. A variety of other codes can also be used, some utilizing things like the length of pauses or insignificant seeming gestures and body language in addition to or instead of verbal cues. [3]

In some such cases there really is no need to develop a code at all. A confederate can simply sit in the audience or on the sides of the performance and mouth or otherwise signal what you wish to know. If anyone should question why you are frequently accompanied by the same people, you can simply tell them that in order for your awesome, barely controllable powers to function, you must be comfortable. Having your friends around helps you remain comfortable. By the way, whatever you do, when you are seeking fame and fortune and publicity of all sorts, you must take care to keep your confederates from being photographed or otherwise noticed by the media. Like the secret agents that they are, their anonymity helps guarantee your success.

Clearly, the system of codes shown in Addendum 4-1 is complex and difficult to learn. It was designed and used by performers who demonstrated mentalism as an important part of their living. Nevertheless, simpler, easier-to-learn codes can be utilized for a variety of purposes. For example, George Estabrooks, a psychologist, once attempted to produce an absolutely cheatproof environment for a telepathy experiment that he wished to conduct. For the experiment, test subjects would use a regular deck of playing cards, but the experiment would only focus on the experimenter's ability to send or receive the color of the card (red or black). The experiment would be based on the subject's ability to get a score higher than 50 percent. To ensure security, the subjects were in different but adjoining rooms, where they could not see each other. Guesses and all other necessary signals were recorded electronically.

Estabrooks was amazed and frustrated when a pair of subjects came and bet him the cost of a dinner that they could successfully cheat. After the subjects guessed the color of 52 cards correctly, winning the dinner, he scoured the laboratory trying to find some suitably complex signaling apparatus, without success. Ultimately he gave up, bribed the subjects with a pair of theater tickets, and learned their technique.

The subjects began with the arbitrary assumption that all odd numbered cards were red and all even numbered cards were black. When the cards were not the color they expected them to be, the sender would cough, scrape his chair a short distance across the floor, drop something, or through some other unobtrusive means make a noise that the receiver could hear on the other side of the double-sided doors. [4]

Telephone Trick

This is a very old telepathy trick, and many feel that it is best for fake psychics to avoid, as it simply looks too much like a magic trick. In other words, if it looks like a trick, acts like a trick, and smells like a trick, then the audience might start catching on that it is a trick. Ultimately, this will lead them to begin looking for the gimmick instead of being awed by your incredible powers. Nevertheless, it's kind of a neat little trick, so it seems worth presenting here. Besides, if you're using these things to educate the public as to how easy it is to recreate telepathic "miracles" artificially, then this may be just the effect that you wish to produce.

You, the psychic that is, announce that you can telepathically transmit signals to a friend of yours with a great deal of success. Obviously, you explain, this must be because of some sort of mysterious bond that exists between the two of you. Don't hesitate to elaborate on this. Although your friend is not present, you can demonstrate this effect easily enough by calling him on the telephone and transmitting to him a picture of a common object such as a coin. You announce that your friend will receive a vivid picture of the coin. Your friend is, of course, a carefully trained confederate.

You call him and say, "I am sending you an image. Are you preparing to receive it?" This is the cue for your friend to begin the trick by slowly and clearly listing the different kinds of coins in order, going from lowest to highest. He starts by saying, "Penny, nickel, dime, quarter," and so on. When he gets to a coin of the proper value, then you interrupt with some innocuous statement. "Good," you say, "These people are skeptical of our telepathic link." Although you never said that it was a coin, you and your confederate always use coins, so this doesn't need to be specified.

As the confederate now knows the value of the coin, next comes the year. This is done in two steps—first the decade, then the year. The confederate begins with a suitable decade such the 1940s—forty, fifty, sixty, seventy, etc. Interrupt him immediately after the appropriate decade is reached, once again by saying something innocuous such as "Good" or "Have you received it yet?"

It is unlikely that you'll get a coin older than that. If such an event does happen, then you should come up with a valid sounding excuse to refuse it, or you and your confederate can do older coins after you go through the newer ones. Decide in advance how you will handle it.

Next, after the decade and the value of the coin have been determined, your confederate should segue immediately into the appropriate year of the decade by reciting one, two, three, four, and so on, with zero last. When he reaches the proper number, you can interrupt with something like, "All right, then you've received it?"

Hand the phone to one of the people who are watching. Your confederate will then say to them something like, "I'm not sure, but I get this image of a 1978 nickel. Is that correct?"

Of course, it is. After all, you just told him it was! By the way, don't ever let the audience know that you are only prepared to do this with coins.

Human Probability Studies

The human mind does not work in an entirely random manner. (Generally speaking, anyway. I do know individuals who I swear must be an exception to this statement.) Rather, it develops patterns of thought. If people are asked or encouraged to come up with something at random—be it a number, a letter, or whatever—over time the same "random" numbers or letters will come up again and again. Magicians, and mentalists in particular, take advantage of this fact to produce spectacular effects. [5]

These often take the form of "thought transmission experiments." The performer will announce that he will transmit messages to the audience in order to test their telepathic ability. He will then establish some parameters for the number. For example, he will state that it is a number between 1 and 50 and that the digits don't repeat. By these two simple parameters, the mentalist has guided the thought processes of the bulk of his audience. He knows that when choosing a number between 1 and 50, most people will choose somewhere near the high end.

Similarly, there are certain means by which a performer can guide the choices of his audience. For instance, if he begins by stating, "Choose a number, any number, between 1 and 5, no, let's make it between 1 and 10," then the number will almost always be between 6 and 10, and only in rare cases will the number be 10 itself. Similarly, for one reason or another, to most people the number 7 seems more random than the number 8 (although logic naturally dictates otherwise). So guess 7. If 7 is not correct, then ask what the number was. If it is between 5 and 9 inclusive, then you are only one or two off. Announce the fact as if this closeness is significant. (See Addendum 4-2 for more on this.)

Transmitting Symbols

This same sort of effect will work for symbols and shapes as well. Here's an old trick that still works. Announce to the audience that you are going to telepathically send them the image of a pair of interlocked shapes, with one inside the other, and that you wish them to be prepared to receive it. State that, "To ensure that this is a valid test, you will not use a square. After all, a square is just too easy and common a shape to use." Then, when the audience is ready, you announce your telepathic transmission.

"How many of you received an image of a triangle inside a circle?"

The bulk of the people in the audience will probably respond affirmatively, much to their own amazement. Then ask how many received an image of a circle inside a triangle? Tell them that this is also close enough to count as a "hit."

The effect is based on the fact that the triangle and the circle are the most commonly thought of shapes after a square. After all, how many people in that audience think you will be sending them a symbol of a rhombus in a tetrahedron? How many even know what that means? I most certainly don't.

CLAIRVOYANCE STUNTS

Clairvoyance, or "distant viewing" as it is sometimes known, is the alleged power of the human mind

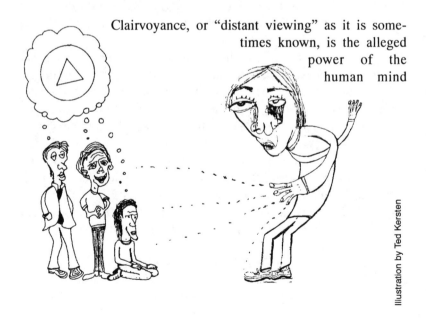

Illustration by Ted Kersten

78

to see things in places or at distances where it would normally be physically impossible to see them.

As with everything else, there are several methods by which this can be hoaxed or simulated. Many of these can be summarized as "peeking when the chance presents itself" and thus are difficult to systemize. Therefore, the first step for one who wishes to produce clairvoyant effects is to simply remain alert and study his or her environment carefully for such opportunities. In other words, if you wish people to think that you are clairvoyant, then you should cheat, cheat, cheat and peek, peek, peek! If such opportunities do not present themselves, and if you have established a reputation as a psychic through other means, then you may simply bow out, announcing that your powers of clairvoyance do not seem to be functioning today. If done properly, such excuses can add to your reputation just as much as a successful demonstration!

Nevertheless, if you're going to tell people that you are clairvoyant, then it would be nice to have some idea of how to fake such things. Here are a few of the methods by which this can be done.

Mirrors

Mirrors and other reflective surfaces are extremely useful for peeking at things from unexpected angles. One of the most useful mirrors for this purpose is the small convex reflective mirror that you can buy at auto parts stores. These come in a variety of sizes and are intended to be attached to a rearview mirror, where the concave surface can help the driver see a wide range of objects.

A small mirror of this sort is surprisingly cheap. My 2-inch-diameter one cost about $1.10, plus tax. It's nice and small and fits snugly in the palm of your hand, where it's easy to conceal. It can also be stored in your pocket, where, unless you wear very snug jeans, it shouldn't leave any embarrassing bulges.

One use for such a mirror is that you can place it in the palm of your hand, cover your eyes like a small child playing hide and seek, and then spin around with your back turned to the object that you aren't supposed to be looking at. You can then peek and see it anyway! Remember, if you wish to be a fake psychic you must cheat, and when it comes to clairvoyance, this means to peek whenever possible.

Do you remember Pee Wee Herman? I confess, I never properly appreciated him, but Pee Wee Herman was a spastic-seeming comedian who kind of flopped around on stage acting infantile and foolish, getting great laughs in the process. Back at the ambulance service where I used to work, everybody else loved him. Unfortunately for all concerned, Pee Wee's career took a sudden nose-dive when he was caught exposing himself in an adult movie theater somewhere down south, and although this confirmed his position as a role model among ambulance attendants, it hurt his standing among children and their parents. Oops!

Well, Pee Wee had this routine where he would tape mirrors onto the tops of his shoes about where the laces are and use them to look up women's dresses so that he could see their panties. There's no reason, outside of half a dozen legal statutes and several social mores, that you can't do this too. Or better yet, put the mirrors in a less obvious place so that people won't notice them so quickly. One suggestion is to tape a small mirror onto the back side of the heel of your shoe. Or you can get a very shiny steel- or aluminum-headed thumbtack and stick it in the proper place on your shoe. Alternatively, you can stick the tack in the end of a cigarette and place it in your mouth. Not only will this allow you to carry a mirror around sight unseen, but having a cigarette hanging out of your mouth is so wonderfully unhealthy and politically incorrect that it is still one of the most effective ways ever to offend self-righteous pricks!

But back to peeking. As a true voyeur should know, nearly any reflective object can be used to peek at one's fellow humans. Reflective surfaces are everywhere! Some common examples are dead TV screens, kitchen knives and other silverware (who can possibly forget the image of Wyonna Rider reflected on that large butcher knife in the classic motion picture *Heathers,* one of my all-time favorite films), dark coffee or tea, shiny book covers (you can often get away with placing a suitable volume on a coffee table, where, like most coffee table books, it will then be ignored), and shoplifting detection mirrors. A spilled drink might even provide a makeshift mirror in some circumstances, or, if you're as classy some of the people I used to hang out with in college, you could always spill beer all over the floor and then try and do a Pee Wee Herman up your date's dress. And don't forget, if you buy your 2-inch concave mirrors at the auto store, they usually have a sticky piece of tape on the back to aid in fastening to the rearview mirror. There's no reason why you couldn't use this to your advantage; just don't get caught!

Reading Envelopes

Clairvoyants are known for being able to read items inside sealed envelopes. Here are some techniques by which you can produce this effect.

The first method, and one of the most impressive, is the "one ahead" method. It is used when a performer wishes to show that he can read the contents of a large number of envelopes. The audience is instructed to write what they wish, perhaps a question to the great psychic himself, on a piece of paper, place it in an envelope, and seal it. The envelopes are then collected and placed in a bowl or similar container. The performer holds up the first envelope, maybe places it on his forehead for effect, then answers the question. He then opens the envelope and reads the question out loud to confirm his ability. He repeats the process, going through the entire stack of envelopes and giving the audience suitable, if somewhat vague, answers to all of their questions.

The trick is done as follows: *the performer is always working one envelope ahead of himself.* For example, he will invent the first question, and then open the first envelope. This question from the first, now opened envelope will be presented as if it were inside the second, still sealed envelope. The performer will answer the question he has already read while pretending that he is, in fact, reading a question that is inside the sealed envelope in his hand. As the envelopes are held up, out of sight of the audience, the trick works fairly well.

The one-ahead trick is one of the simplest, most reliable, and most spectacular methods to read the content of sealed envelopes, but there are others. For instance, you can simply hold an envelope up to the light in order to see through it. Marking an envelope sometimes can help you keep track of what is inside it. In some cases, if you're alert and the situation presents itself, you can make use of distinctions between envelopes, such as the way they are sealed and the placement of staples and tape, if any.

Sometimes a psychic will write down his "clairvoyant images" instead of speaking them out loud. One way to take advantage of this method is to simply *pretend* to write down the "vision" beforehand. Later, when the envelope has been opened, you secretly write down what you see. The easiest way to do this is with a little device called a "nail writer." This is, essentially, a little pencil that the audience can't see. The cheapest and best way to devise a nail writer is to take a small piece of some kind of suitable putty or glue and place a short piece of pencil lead under your thumbnail with the tip projecting slightly so that you can write with it. There are also commercial devices available at magic shops that are, in effect, false thumb tips with a pencil lead sticking out. They look less realistic and cost more than the do-it-yourself method, though, so I don't recommend them.

Using a nail writer is easy. Pretend to write your answer on the paper before you know the answer. Later, when you do know the answer, simply scratch it on the paper with your nail writer.

ADDENDUM 4-1

REPRESENTATIVE SAMPLES FROM
A MENTALIST'S PERFORMANCE CODE

The following are portions of a mentalist's code from the turn of the century. Through the use of codes such as these, an assistant could transmit a great deal of information to a performer. Although the system was complex and took a great deal of memorization on the part of the performers, this made it more difficult for the audience to determine the methods by which the information was transmitted.

ALPHABET

A = H	O = V
B = T	P = J
C = S	Q = W
D = G	R = M
E = F	S = N
F = E	T = P
G = A	U = Look
H = I	V = Y
I = B	W = R
J = L	X = See This
K = Pray	Y = Q
L = C	Z = Hurry
N = D	Hurry Up = repeat the last
M = O	letter

By using this table, an assistant could transmit a spelling of a word to the performer. The letter in the code would be used as the first letter in a sentence. For example, if the assistant were holding a bracelet with the name "Anna" engraved on it, he might say to the performer, "Here is a name. Do you see it? Hurry Up! Have you got it?" This phrase, or others like it, spells out "A-N-repeat-A." or "ANNA" to a listener who knows the code.

Yet this portion of the code is only one small part of the entire system. The section on numbers is reproduced below.

NUMBERS

1 = Say	7 = Please or Pray
2 = Be, Look, or Let	8 = Are or Ain't
3 = Can or Can't	9 = Now
4 = Do or Don't	10 = Tell
5 = Will or Won't	0 = Hurry or Come
6 = What	

The above number code is used in a manner quite similar to the letter code. For example, to secretly communicate the number 1,234 to a performer, an assistant would say a phrase such as, "Say the number. Look at it. Can you see it? Do you know what it is?" By using the code word in each sentence, he would communicate the number to the performer.

There were many later charts in which the numbers were used to communicate more complex ideas to the performer.

COLORS

1 = White	5 = Red
2 = Black	6 = Green
3 = Blue	7 = Yellow
4 = Brown	8 = Gray

In the above chart, each of the common colors has a number. If the assistant were to say, "Say the color!" to the performer, the performer would know that he meant the number one color, or white. If the assistant said something such as "Please tell us the color," it would indicate the number seven color, or yellow.

Metal and the settings charts could be used in a similar manner to describe various aspects of jewelry. As identifying and describing various pieces of the audience's jewelry was an important part of the act, such codes were needed to make the performance work.

METALS

1 = Gold
2 = Silver
3 = Brass
4 = Copper
5 = Lead

6 = Iron
7 = Tin
8 = Platina
9 = Steel

THE SETTINGS

1 = Diamond
2 = Ruby
3 = Pearl
4 = Amethyst
5 = Onyx

6 = Garnet
7 = Emerald
8 = Turquoise
9 = Carbuncle
10 = Topaz

By now, it should be clear that "Can you tell us the metal?" meant it was made of brass, and "Are you able to tell us the stone?" meant that the stone was turquoise.

As the range of details that could be shared was nearly limitless, there were a number of charts that could be used to indicate all sorts of information. Miscellaneous articles were divided into sets for purposes of identification. By using the right introductory phrase, the assistant indicated what sort of information would be presented.

FIRST SET

"What article is this?"

1 = Handkerchief	6 = Basket
2 = Neckerchief	7 = Beet
3 = Bag	8 = Comforter
4 = Glove	9 = Headdress
5 = Purse	10 = Fan

For example, if an assistant said, "What article is this? Will you say?" it indicates that the article is on the chart above in the number five position and hence a purse.

SECOND SET

"What is this?"

1 = Watch	6 = Necklace
2 = Bracelet	7 = Ring
3 = Guard	8 = Rosary
4 = Chain	9 = Cross
5 = Breast pin	10 = Charm

THIRD SET

"What may this be?"

1 = Hat	6 = Muff
2 = Cap	7 = Cape
3 = Bonnet	8 = Boa
4 = Cuff	9 = Inkstand
5 = Collar	10 = Mucilage

The charts above are only a small portion of the system. The entire system is reproduced in *Magic: Stage Illusions, Special Effects, and Trick Photography* and is taken from that work.

ADDENDUM 4-2

SOME GUIDELINES AS TO HOW PEOPLE CHOOSE RANDOM NUMBERS

When most people are asked to choose a random number, they tend to choose the following:

1) Odd numbers.
2) Nonrepeating digits.
3) 25 is relatively common.

Source: James Randi, personal communication.

ENDNOTES

1   It should be noted that these terms, and virtually all others referring to alleged parapsychological phenomena, are frequently misused. I've recently noticed advertisements for 1-900 clairvoyant Tarot card readers! Technically, I suppose this means that they use their clairvoyant powers to read Tarot cards that are hidden from their view.

2   Actually, not too long ago, one prominent televangelist used a hidden microphone while his wife sent him messages about audience members' personal lives on a radio transmitter. Through these messages he would obtain otherwise unobtainable information that would be presented to his audience as an insight sent from God. For the full details of this bizarre, fascinating, and disturbing story and its discovery by the magician James Randi, see *The Faith Healers* by James Randi. Such a radio transmitter also played a prominent part in the entertaining motion picture *Leap of Faith*, which featured Steve Martin as a corrupt televangelist.

3   In Booth's *Psychic Paradoxes*, a brief history of some mentalist performers, their acts, and the sorts of codes that they used is presented.

4   Neher, *The Psychology of Transcendence,* pp. 142–143.

5   One performer who uses such things prominently in his act goes by the name of Kreskin. Known by detractors as "the ambiguous Kreskin," there is no doubt that he is a talented performer with an excellent understanding of human psychology and behavior. Critics complain, however, that Kreskin seems unable to decide whether he is claiming to be psychic or not. First he'll announce that he's not, then later make an ambivalent statement that he just might be. Oh well.

Part 2
UFOs

Like Totally Unbelievable Encounters, Dude!

The Art of Rolling Your Own UFO Photos

"Yet surely there's more among the heavens and the earth than we can imagine."

"Oh no doubt."

"And you cannot say that our mundane existence is the only sort of existence imaginable."

"Of course not."

"In fact, I once saw this picture where . . ."

"A picture?"

"Yes, a picture is worth a thousand words, you know."

"That may be, but everyone knows that a thousand words can still tell a thousand lies . . ."

Although there is a great deal of controversy in today's UFO scene, there are some things that can be agreed on. First, there is a lot of stuff in the sky. Second, some of this stuff is quite interesting, and much of it appears quite strange, even bizarre, to an observer. Third, it is fairly obvious to an impartial observer that most UFO incidents have been hyped up, promoted, and distorted by hysteria, overexcited witnesses, or various overzealous media factions. Fourth, the overwhelming majority of prominent UFO investigators will agree that at least some of the other prominent UFO investigators out there are not only grossly incompetent but consciously lie and distort facts for one reason or another.

Be this as it may, mysterious lights in the sky hold a great fascination for many and have, in some circles, taken on a mystical significance. To such people, the lights in the sky are not just lights—they are something "more." Popular theories include spaceships from extraterrestrial civilizations, time machines from the future, and mysterious craft from other planes of reality. To the more extreme born-again Christians, UFOs are demons sent by Satan to delude us in the Endtimes before the imminent Rapture. To some neo-Nazis, UFOs are emissaries sent by the advanced surviving Nazi civilization inside of the Hollow Earth. [1]

Nevertheless, among "serious" UFOlogists, spaceships from an advanced extraterrestrial civilization are the explanation of choice. Of course, I am in no position to refute this idea, but I will state that it has always seemed to me that a strong element of rumormongering runs through these claims. For example, first there's a light in the sky. Then, with no further evidence, it is a spaceship in the sky. Then it's a spaceship flown by aliens. Then

it's a spaceship flown by an alien race known as "the Greys." And so on, until finally it's a spaceship flown by an alien race known as the Greys who are from the star system Pleiades, and the federal government knows this but is suppressing the evidence because they don't want us to panic over their uncovering of the Greys' secret plan to conduct genetic experiments on us by using their mind-control technology.

As for the evidence people use to come to this conclusion, not only does it fail to convince most scientists, but it also fails to convince the "UFOs are Satanic demons" people, the "Nazi saucers from the Hollow Earth" people, and the "UFOs as time machines" people.

That's okay, though. Scientists, fundamentalists, neo-Nazis, and armchair time travelers are universally known for being tough to convince. Besides, they are not the primary market for UFO photographs. No matter what they say to the contrary, for the foreseeable future, there will always be a host of magazines, TV shows, and paperback book companies that will be clamoring for a peek at almost any halfway decent UFO photo. Therefore, let us present a variety of methods to make UFO photos.

According to at least one source, serious UFO investigators attempt to divide mysterious photos of unexplained aerial phenomena into the following categories. [2]

- Misidentifieds
- Optical or photographically generated misidentifieds
- Natural aerial phenomena
- Hoaxes
- Unidentified

Out of these categories, it is the "unidentified" photos, or the ones that are considered to be truly unsolvable, that UFO enthusiasts find the most exciting and frequently promote as evidence of visiting spaceships.

The others are all more mundane. Misidentifieds are everyday objects seen or photographed in such a way so that they become difficult or impossible to identify correctly. For example, it is not uncommon for aircraft to be misidentified by viewers as something more mysterious. If the aircraft is of an unusual sort or appearance, then this is particularly common. Blimps or advertising planes with dragging banners or strange lights are particularly likely targets to be reported as UFOs by large numbers of people, especially if seen at night from a strange angle in such a way that their lights cannot be viewed clearly.

Optical or photographically misidentifieds are unusual pictures accidentally produced due to a problem with the camera, the lighting, the film, or the interactions thereof.

Natural aerial phenomena are ordinary astronomical, meteorological, or other phenomena that appear unusual to a viewer of a photograph. For example, the planet Venus is frequently misperceived as being an airplane or even a spaceship. Phillip J. Klass, a former editor with *Aviation Week and Space Technology,* experienced UFO investigator, and prominent skeptic, has written of how some Second World War B-29 bomber crews attempted to "shoot down" the planet Venus on occasion, believing it to be an enemy aircraft that was following them. [3] Other candidates for misidentified natural aerial phenomena reported as UFOs are the sun and the moon (particularly under unusual conditions), meteorites, unusual clouds, and a variety of mirages.

Hoaxes are, of course, the phenomenon with which we are the most concerned here, and the following are a few of the common means by which such photos can be easily created.

TOSSED OBJECTS

Often, the simplest ways of doing things are best. A quick glance at the following series of photos reveals a method of creating UFO photos that is almost comically simple.

By taking a saucer-shaped object and tossing it into the air, you can easily create a good UFO photograph.

Don't laugh too quickly; the advantages to this method are many. Since you are, in fact, photographing a genuine flying object, there are no strings or visible signs of support waiting to be uncovered. Likewise, there are no signs of trick photography or double exposures that can be discovered. In order to disprove the photograph, an investigator must either identify the object in the photo or determine its size through some very complicated procedures. [4]

A man. A plan. A hubcap! What more could anyone want?

Look! Up in the sky! It's a bird! It's a plane! It's a UFO from the planet Chevy!

Some tips based on experience here:
1. Hubcaps can be surprisingly heavy. Be careful if you throw them, and make sure you don't hit yourself or somebody else.
2. Avoid an area with lots of trees or other items in the background. This technique works best if you can get a clear shot of your object with nothing but sky behind it.
3. If you must use heavy things like hubcaps, sometimes it can help if you throw them from a height such as a roof or ladder. Try not to fall off as you throw the object. If you must fall off, make sure your friend with the camera gets a picture of you plummeting in mid-air, as you may be able to tell people that this is you being sucked upward into the UFO! If you get injured in the fall, and you have insurance, consider sticking to the story, because then

if the company pays your doctor's bills, you can say that they "investigated and verified" your story.

4. Don't get too hung up on the idea of using hubcaps. There are a lot of lighter, less dangerous, more easily obtainable items that are just as usable. It was discovered, for example, that one particularly effective UFO was a strange-looking rubber chew toy for a dog that was covered with aluminum foil. It was light, it was easy to toss, it was virtually indestructible, and if it hit something it caused no damage.

MODELS

The classic method of faking a UFO picture is to use a model. You simply toss it into the air as described above, but unless your

This "UFO" is actually a dog's cheap rubber chew toy wrapped in aluminum foil. It was quite possible to obtain good height and distance using this highly complicted device.

Another shot of the same dog toy. We could throw the rubber toy as hard as we wanted without worrying too much about damaging nearby houses and people (including ourselves—something easy to understand if you've ever tried tossing a hubcap into the air while standing underneath it).

model is pretty sturdy or you come up with some fairly elaborate means to cushion the landing, it will fall apart after a few shots. Instead, you can simply hang the thing from a pole on a thread. The obvious problem with this method is that the strings might show up in a photo.

You can build your model from virtually anything you'd like. After all, nobody knows what a true UFO looks like, or, even if they think they do, then it should be a pretty simple matter to convince them that you've found a new type. You can also simply purchase a commercially available model kit. Testors makes one of these, and, bizarrely enough, it's "guaranteed authentic."

DOUBLE EXPOSURES

Double exposures are another classic method of making UFO photos. As most people know, a double exposure is when a person

UFO on a stick. Actually, this is a commercially produced model kit hung on an old broomstick.

This photo illustrates some common, easy-to-avoid mistakes. 1) Use of the earth, rather than the sky, as background makes the model look small; 2) the string is clearly visible; 3) the pole from which the model is hung leaves an obvious shadow on the model.

In these two photos, the string was hidden in different ways.

takes a picture twice on the same piece of film. It used to be that this was easily done on most cameras. In fact, it was frequently done by accident, resulting in botched photos and angry consumers, so today most cameras are built in such a way that it's quite difficult to take a double exposure with them.

Not being an expert on cameras, I do not wish to discuss how you may take double exposures with any particular brand of camera. You can determine this for yourself. Obtain assistance from a camera store, photographer, or other source, if necessary.

Instead, a second, easier method is to simply expose the entire roll of film twice. To do this, you take a series of photos. When you are done, remove the film as normal. You will discover that the little tab is now tucked inside the roll. To reinsert the entire roll of film, you must find a way to pull the loading tab out. The simplest way that I've found to do this is to get your friendly neighborhood photo developer to do it for you. Since pulling the tab from the canister is the first step in removing the film for development, they're experts at this and have special machines that do it. (These

This photo is a double exposure produced according to the instructions in the text.

The above UFO photo was produced in two minutes by simply scratching directly on the emulsion of the negative. I've seen better photos where the scratched image was touched up with colored inks.

machines are surprisingly elaborate and large and do not seem to be suitable for home use.)

The developers tell me that if this won't work, then there are other means to remove that tab. You can insert a wet piece of film into the camera and use it to pull out the exposed film. At this point, it's a simple matter to reinsert the roll of film into the camera.

Of course, if you have a friend with a darkroom for film developing, then he can make double exposures for you quite easily and should know how to do it. Some commercial photographers can be hired for this purpose, but they would probably charge a lot, and where's the fun in hiring somebody to fake a simple UFO photograph for you?

When making double exposures of UFOs, the simplest way to make the UFO image is to use a bright light. If done correctly, the light will appear as a shiny, bright object that appears to be floating in the sky.

Making such a light is relatively simple. Find a dark place such as

SUPPRESSED BY THE
"SECRET GOVERNMENT"
CENSORED BY THE MEDIA

Our 144 page fully illustrated research report is guaranteed to shake common sensibility.

Includes shocking information on:

✓ Free Energy ✓ UFOS
✓ AREA 51 ✓ NIKOLA TESLA

Prepared by "Commander X" (a former military intelligence operative). here are Top-Secret revelations about astounding new inventions being tested by U.S. Government and private citizens.

a basement. Get a flashlight and some sort of small hole to narrow the beam (most flashlight beams are too broad and leave too large an image). We used an old Dolly Parton record (remember records?) bought at a garage sale. It seemed like a better use for it than to actually listen to it again.

PICTURES ON GLASS

A surprisingly easy method to fake a UFO photo is to simply place something on a piece of glass and then take a picture of it. I first did this at the age of nine, believe it or not, by taping a dime and some paper on the good ol' living room window and then photographing the result. It wowed my classmates, even though one pompous jackass (who later went on to be Key Club president) insisted that it was simply a C-130 from the local air national guard base.

Using windows is the so-called "vertical method." There's also the horizontal method, where you simply place a pane of glass or an old window flat and then take a picture from underneath it. We've discovered that taking the photos at an angle distorts the circular effect of the objects used (coins will do quite well) and makes the

The author (in need of a
haircut and some exercise,
as always) produced the
photograph at right using
this old window pane and
some spare pocket change.

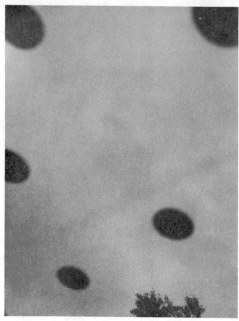

shape appear more realistic. The photo on page 104 was made in this way by crawling underneath an old window pane propped between two chairs.

Although all of the above techniques will produce a passable UFO photo that is perfectly good for everyday use and joking around and most likely can even be sold to some of the poorer UFO magazines (the bad quality of some published UFO photos has to be seen to be believed!), they will not fool most experts who use advanced techniques to determine the authenticity of such photos. Before you try to pass something off as real, make a solid effort to determine how the experts will verify it.

COMPUTER SUPERIMPOSITIONS

Soon, models and solid objects will be completely passé and unnecessary for trick photography. Like so much else, computers are taking over the field. In fact, it has been predicted that we will soon enter an age when computerized trick photography is so advanced that photographic proof will be worthless. Fake will be indistinguishable from reality. Disturbingly, the same techniques shown here will be able to be utilized to distort and create images on the daily news. In effect, the verifiability of any reported event will have gone full circle and returned to the days of eyewitness accounts before photos could provide proof of an event or scene having taken place.

A friend of mine makes such computer superimpositions all the time. Although his computer skills strike a near computer illiterate such as myself as quite advanced (I lean on him a lot for technical support during my various projects), he assures me that, in fact, his skills are really nothing out of the ordinary. The software he uses is Graphic Workshop, which is standard with Microsoft Windows, and a photo enhancement program that he obtained easily as shareware. He insists that others with access to more advanced software and images could make extremely sophisticated images just as easily. [5]

This photo was created using computer software. The golf course was photographed in the normal manner. The photo was then scanned into Adobe Photoshop using a modestly priced image scanner. The designer then created the UFO using the "tools" in Photoshop. Note the clever addition of the shadow on the ground as well.

ADDENDUM 5-1

RAY PALMER AND "THE SHAVER MYSTERY"

One of the continuing fascinations of the world of the paranormal, particularly for a cynical skeptic such as myself, is the endless array of extreme personality types pulling off audacious hoaxes. Ray Palmer is a perfect example.

Perhaps a partial explanation for Ray Palmer's motivations lies in his childhood. Tragically, it is reported that at the tender age of 7, he was run over by a truck, leaving him hunchbacked, permanently deformed, and subject to periodic bouts of great pain. This is most likely true, as there are photographs to back it up and little reason to lie. As for all other facts concerning the life, times, and amazing career of Ray Palmer, questions soon arise, and records contradict one another.

He was born in either 1908, 1910, or 1911. He grew to be either 4 feet or else 4 feet 8 inches tall. His shift from fanatical science fiction fan to professional came when he sold his first story to a low-budget pulp magazine at the age of either 16 or 20, once again depending on which source you use. It is said that he once submitted a story, his second, 99 times, receiving rejection after rejection, before it finally sold on the hundredth.

In any event, his next big move was from writing to editing the low-budget pulp science fiction magazines that dotted the literary landscape of that pretelevision era. During his 40-year career, Palmer proved himself more than an able and competent editor. As one of his colleagues stated, "In these times of drab and unconvincing falsehood, there is still something to be thankful for. A Palmer promotion has the touch of genius. It has zing, sparkle, and true showmanship. It can be spotted a mile away by the bright lights. The thing to do is sit back and enjoy it." [6]

Such zest and aplomb was shown with the so-called "Shaver Mystery." In 1943, *Amazing Stories* received an unusual letter in the mail. It claimed to provide, in detail, the secrets of the long lost Atlantean alphabet. It came from a man by the name of Richard Shaver. The facts concerning the life of Shaver are almost in as much dispute as those of Palmer. Some sources state that Shaver had been hospitalized for schizophrenic delusions of a paranoid nature, and this seems quite believable. In a manner typical of the writings of schizophrenics, the letter went on to state that by using the Atlantean alphabet, one could determine underlying meaning, and he included strange religious references and the peculiar sort of seemingly irrelevant symbolic correlations that such people seem to find so meaningful.

Shaver, not surprisingly, gave several different versions throughout his life of how he had received the details of the alphabet. The most frequently repeated seems to be that he had received the messages telepathically from an electric welding tool that he had been using. As he already believed himself telepathic and able to receive thoughts from all the people around him, he found this only mildly surprising. Shaver believed that an alien race called the Dero were sending him these messages using the welder as a telepathic "teleradio." [7]

Naturally, being a communicative race, they sent Shaver a wide variety of messages describing their life and racial history in great detail. The Dero, it seems, were evil dwarfs who lived inside the Earth. Their enemies were a good race known as the Titans. They had existed for thousands upon thousands of years, and their wars had rocked the prehistoric earth, ultimately becoming part of mankind's mythology.

When Shaver's letter first arrived at *Amazing Stories*, a junior editor, not surprisingly, threw it in the garbage, dismissing it as an obvious nut letter. Palmer fished it out of the trash, chided the editor as lacking in vision, and printed it in his magazine, with the explanation to his readers that such a piece, if true, could necessitate the entire rewriting of the history of mankind. *Amazing Stories*, he explained, was morally obligated to print such a monumental tome and requested readers' assistance in getting to the truth of this great mystery they had uncovered.

Predictably, the article caused a great deal of reader response and interest. Although much of it was hostile, calling Palmer names for running such trash, a surprising amount came from readers who claimed they had knowledge of the Dero and wished to share it with like-minded people. In time, the Shaver Mystery led to a great boost in the sales of *Amazing Stories*, and soon virtually every issue included something on it. Future details included such things as descriptions of Dero robots, UFOs, and the claimed entrance to the hollow Earth somewhere around the North Pole.

Eventually, Palmer came to realize that there was a great market for this sort of thing and began publishing his own "nonfiction" UFO and paranormal magazines. The most popular of these was undoubtedly *FATE*, a magazine that is still published monthly today. Palmer passed away in 1977. [8]

ADDENDUM 5-2

THE CAREER OF GEORGE ADAMSKI

George Adamski was born in Poland in 1891, but at an early age he emigrated with his family to the United States. Although lacking in formal education, he seems to have had a varied background, working as a cavalry soldier on the Mexican border, a flour worker, a concrete contractor, and a maintenance man at Yellowstone National Park. He seems to have settled down in California, where he made much of his living teaching others various schools of mysticism, at least some of which were of his own creation. One of his schools, The Royal Order of Tibet, made a great deal of money, as it had the special license needed to produce wine during Prohibition. Of this Adamski is quoted as having said, "I made enough wine for all of Southern California," and he is said to have remarked that if it weren't for the repeal of Prohibition, "I wouldn't have had to get into this saucer crap." [9]

In any event, it was through flying saucers that Adamski made his name. According to Adamski, he saw his first saucer in 1946, but eventually he went beyond merely seeing them. Instead, beginning in the early 1950s, he began describing his frequent contacts with the "Space Brothers." The Space Brothers, at least as Adamski described them, were much like humans, only much more advanced and benevolent. They came from a wide variety of planets. Adamski himself was visited by people from Mars, Venus, and Saturn. Like everyone else presumed by society at large to be of any importance in the 1950s, the Space Brothers were universally Caucasian, although they could be of either sex. Surprisingly for the time, some had long hair. They communicated with Adamski by either telepathy or English, depending on their mood or the occasion.

Adamski described his visits with the Space Brothers in a pair of books, *Flying Saucers Have Landed,* which was only 60 pages long, and *Inside the Spaceships,* which was a full 219 pages. [10] These books describe the wide variety of contacts that Adamski claimed to have had with the aliens. The aliens, who frequently met him in cafes and hotel lobbies, encouraged Adamski to urge his fellow Earth people to cease the development of nuclear weapons and to strive to get along with one another. They would take him for long trips throughout the solar system and even went so far, according to the second book, as to take him on a trip to the dark side of the moon where, unlike the later Apollo astronauts, he met lots of friendly Space Brothers and saw the sights, including cities, animals, and vegetation.

Naturally, a lot of people have found flaws and inconsistencies in Adamski's stories. His photos of flying saucers are regarded as fakes, and witnesses to his alleged encounters with the Space Brothers and their ships have frequently accused him of telling lies or at the least exaggerating details. [11]

Nevertheless, Adamski's legacy lives on. His teachings inspired a host of imitators and a variety of strange saucer cults. Although few recognize Adamski, preferring to claim that their messages have come direct from the space beings themselves, the influence is definitely there. [12] Few informed people can deny that George Adamski was not only a liar and a rogue but that he was also a man whose ideas helped lead to many of today's UFO beliefs.

ENDNOTES

1   This idea may be losing steam. Its most prominent promoter, Ernst Zundel, has moved onto other things. Zundel has made a career out of promoting a variety of fringe, neo-Nazi theories. Among these is the   saucer/Hollow Earth idea. Disturbingly enough, Zundel is finding that another topic that he promotes, that the Holocaust never occurred (Holocaust revisionism, or Holocaust denial), is starting to be taken more seriously by some people who do not consider themselves racists. In an effort to make himself more palatable to such people, Zundel has stopped publishing UFO-related materials and now admits that he made them all up. This previous lie brings his entire credibility into question.

2   "Is a Picture Worth a Thousand Words" in *Phenomenon: Forty Years of Flying Saucers.*

3   *UFO Abductions: A Dangerous Game*, p. 13. By the way, Mr. Klass's reputation for debunking and criticizing UFO reports has reached a point where it is possible to buy dart boards with his face on them at many UFO conventions. Klass owns one himself and keeps it next to his writing desk.

4   To get an overview of these methods, read *Camera Clues* by Joe Nickell.

5   It's worth mentioning that on the Internet and in various bulletin boards, computer buffs frequently swap GIFs or Graphic Image Files. These are files that can be used to create pictures using other software. Many of these are pornographic in nature, and nude photos of singers and actresses are quite common.

    A friend of mine has built up quite a collection of these. (Hey, I never claimed that my friends were classy!) He bragged to me that he had nude GIFs of virtually every singer and actress available and begged me to try and stump him. Challenged and after much pressuring, I strove for the obscure and finally asked if he had one of a very talented female musician who sings country music without the bitter redneck aftertaste. Much to my surprise he promptly found one. Of course, many of these GIFs consist of celebrity heads computer-grafted on noncelebrity bodies. So if there are nude GIFs available of actresses and actors who have never in their lives posed nude, then there is no way for anyone to know whether the image is authentic or not. The message to hoaxers is obvious.

6   As credited to P.W. Fairman, a colleague of Palmers, in 1952. Source: *Subterranean Worlds*, p. 134.

7   It is common among persons with untreated schizophrenia to believe that they are receiving telepathic communications from electrical devices.

8   Sources for this piece include: "The Man Who Invented Flying Saucers: The Story of Ray Palmer," by John Keel in *The Fringes of Reason; Subterranean Worlds: 10,000 Years of Dragons, Dwarfs, the Dead, Lost Races, and UFOs*

from Inside the Earth by Walter Kafton-Mindel; and *Watch the Skies: A Chronicle of the Flying Saucer Myth* by Curtis Peebles.

9   Peebles, *Watch the Skies*, p. 93.

10   Both are still in print today (although combined as one volume) and available from The George Adamski Foundation (where else?) at P.O. Box 1722, Vista, CA 92085.

11   Peebles, pp. 93–99.

12   A pair of good books on saucer cults are Festinger, Riecken, and Schachter's *When Prophecy Fails* (1956, Harper Torchbooks, New York) and Douglas Curran's *In Advance of the Landing: Folk Concepts of Outer Space* (1985, Abbeville Press, New York).

    It should be mentioned that, humorous as they may sound, saucer cults, like any other cult, do have a very serious hard-edged side to them at times. A personal acquaintance of mine, someone who never had the least bit of interest in any of my paranormal and skeptical pursuits, had his marriage split up when his wife ran off, leaving him with three children to care for, and joined a group that was channeling the teachings of the Space Brothers. She explained that preparing for the visit of the Space Brothers and the earthshaking changes they would bring was of much more importance than handling the mundane affairs of her family. He, needless to say, disagreed, but didn't have much say in the matter, as he was a mere Earthling and therefore lacking a certain cosmic perspective. Bizarre as the cause may be, this family's suffering was, and is, not humorous.

Let My People Go! And While You're At It, Keep Off Of My Farm!

Alien Abductions, Crop Circles, and Cattle Mutilations

The pilgrim looked the guru in the eye, his face glowing with contempt. "You stink! You stink! You stink!" he shouted.
"I know I am, but what are you?" replied the guru calmly.
The mystical dialogue continued . . .

Unless one is an astronomer or LSD addict, one can only look at lights in the sky for so long. Therefore, not everything in the field of UFO beliefs involves UFOs per se. In this chapter, we'll look at the peripheral UFO phenomena: alien abductions and crop circles. But first, we must mention cattle mutilations.

An American researcher was shocked by what he heard and saw first-hand on a recent trip to Brazil.

Mutilation, Death and UFOs

CATTLE MUTILATIONS

From time to time, in the United States and elsewhere, cattle get killed. As cattle are valuable, this naturally excites ranchers. An investigation is called for, and sometimes the source of the cow killing remains unsolved. And as in all "unsolved mysteries," speculation can fly.

In time a great sense of mystery surrounding these "cattle mutilations" has appeared, and a modern-day mythology has risen up to provide answers where none existed. An original culprit was UFOs, but when this became passé, Satanic cults were accused. Today, the Satanic cults are no longer the culprit of choice. Instead, cattle mutilations have become a vital part of the "New World Order" furor, as rumors fly of black helicopters under secret control zipping here and there across the landscape committing random acts of bovine butchery wherever they might happen to land. At one point, the hysteria reached a point where a government grant subsidized a study that determined that the overwhelming bulk of the cattle mutilations could in fact be traced to normal causes such as predators of various sorts. Naturally, this mundane answer satisfied nobody ("Government cover up," they cried), and the frenzy continues today.

'Our space alien neighbors are back . . . and they're making our lives miserable!'

WARNING: THIS TRUE-TO-LIFE POSTER MIGHT SCARE YOU WITH IT'S REALISM FROM INSIDE EYEWITNESS ALIEN ENCOUNTERS

ALIEN ENCOUNTERS POSTER

Top Secret Files exposed to reveal this startling authentic rendering of alien sightings.

This Limited Edition 16"x20" FULL COLOR Litho Print by Artist · brings to life alien encounters from those who experienced it first hand. This offer is going fast so order TODAY.

CALL 1-800-

If you'd like to be part of this hysteria, then a) you are a terrible human being and should be ashamed of yourself, and b) you may find our easy process shown in Addendum 6-1 to be of use to you.

ALIEN ABDUCTIONS

In an alien abduction, otherworldly beings in a UFO are alleged to come and abduct a human being (hence the name), do experiments on him and what have you, only then to let him go. In the overwhelming bulk of such cases, there is no evidence of a real abduction, just the testimony of the (generally) upset person who claims to be the abductee. [2] With this being the case, there is nothing to fake for those who wish to do so. Besides, the only way to really make money off of the experience is to sell your story, and these days abduction tales come a dime a dozen. Unless one has great writing or communication skills, there really is nothing to be gained from faking a UFO abduction. [3] And if you've got good communication skills, then surely you have something better to say than a bunch of lies about how you were captured by a flying saucer. Books on abductions do sell, but the truly big money-earning UFO books today tend to come from those few wacky and wild psy-

chologists and psychiatrists who explain how they believe that aliens are abducting their clients. [4] Nevertheless, if you'd like to see some little-known facts about one of the more famous UFO abduction stories, see Addendum 6-2.

Illustration by Ted Kersten

CROP CIRCLES

Crop circles are a mysterious phenomenon in which something comes along and knocks down a circle or other geometric shape in the middle of a field of wheat or other grain. There are a variety of theories as to what could be making these circles, but the most popular ones seem to be alien spaceships, unknown "Earth energies," or bizarre government experiments hidden from the public. Personally, I am a strong proponent of the "bored terrestrial teenagers theory," as crop circles can be easily hoaxed through a variety of means, many of which will be shared here.

Believers have been striving for years to find a way to distinguish "real" crop circles that cannot be explained from "hoaxed" crop circles that can. These standards vary, however, and in any case, seem quite arbitrary. Recently, I attended a UFO conference where a speaker told of how he had discovered a way to differentiate between real and false crop circles by detecting minute changes in their magnetic fields. He claimed this method was accurate. He even believed that his method was so accurate that it could be used to discredit those who had confessed to having hoaxed crop circles in the past when the two contradicted each other. Besides, he insisted, the bulk of people who confessed to having hoaxed a crop circle were usually immature troublemakers or other shady characters who could not be taken seriously and might simply be trying to "explain away" an unknown natural phenomenon. (Apparently he expects only upright, solid citizens to go around hoaxing crop circles in the middle of the night.)

Some guidelines for hoaxing a crop circle are shown in Addendum 6-3. As can be seen, they are rather sketchy. Here, we'll elaborate a little bit upon each step.

Knocking down crops can be done in a variety of ways. None of these will endear you to the person who owns or has grown these crops, so be careful. Better yet, go and do it on your own land or the land of somebody who approves of this sort of thing.

You could wear boards on your feet and knock the crops down.

You could get a bunch of big burly guys like football or rugby players, have them lock arms, have one of them act as a pivot, and then tell the rest of the bunch to run around in circles.

In some areas, particularly in England, crop circle making seems to have become an art, and the circles are taking on more and more elaborate shapes. You may wish to try this yourself by plotting coordinates for different shapes and stomping the crops accordingly. One famous English crop circle maker wears a peculiar little scope made from a pop top hanging over one eye so that he can sight a straight line more easily and accurately. Most likely, any sort of narrow tube and a row of sticks put into the ground can help one plot a nice straight line. A string or rope fastened to a central stake or post can help you be sure that your circle is circular.

There are two other methods that can be used to plot out crop circles. The first is to set up a system of coordinate graphing. Plot the crop circle on a system of small grids on a sheet of paper drawn into squares. Then plot the area of the field into larger squares. Each square on the paper corresponds to a larger square in the field. Use the paper diagram with its marked squares to determine what shape or combination of shapes should be in each area of the field.

The second is to find a way to use a tall chair or lookout post to look down on the workers and direct them. This is a bit complex but in some cases might be useful. Perhaps someone could stand on top of a car and look down and direct the results. [5]

The next level in the process of creating a really good hoaxed crop circle is to make the thing magnetic. This is to confuse and excite the people who believe that real crop circles are magnetically different from other areas of the countryside. To do this, simply take a bunch of iron filings and toss them around the site. If you could find a way to magnetize those filings, then that would really be cool.

You can also make your crop circle radioactive. Now before you panic, we'd better explain that radiation is a bit like body odor. Although it scares people and it's best avoided, in small amounts it won't hurt you too much. Nevertheless, because radiation is so scary, it adds a nice touch to sprinkle something that's just lightly radioactive into the circle in the hopes that somebody will notice. When word gets out that the thing is radioactive, few people are going to ask, "How much?" Instead, they'll just simply assume that no matter how much is there, it's most likely of unnatural origin and definitely something to be terrified of.

You'll need something that is lightly radioactive, easy to get ahold of, and sprinklable. I have been told that two good candidates for this are, believe it or not, road salt designed to produce melting and diet Italian salad dressing. I found this last one difficult to believe, but my sources insist that they are not joking. They say it has something to do with the mineral oil. I don't know. If you have access to a Geiger counter or other radiation-testing device, then you may wish to test this out before you actually use it.

One final point about crop circles. If the media publicizes a crop circle, then a surprisingly large number of people will come to see it. Many of these people will be unbelievably weird. They may wish to sleep in the crop circle or meditate in it or do God knows what else in it. A local farmer had one erupt on his property. A TV station carried a sensationalized story about the incident and within a few days the flow of people got so bad that the farmer felt obligated to plow the damn thing under just to keep them away.

ADDENDUM 6-1

CATTLE MUTILATIONS—THE "E-Z" METHOD

STEP ONE—Find a dead cow that's been all messed up and left in a field.

STEP TWO—Find someone who talks more than they should and whisper something exciting in their ear, such as, "You know, don't tell anyone this, but that cow has had all of its blood drained," or "You know, don't tell anyone this, but there were men in white suits here last night from a government agency," or "You know, don't tell anyone this, but my cousin Delbert is an MIT student, and he told me that those marks all over the cattle look just like they came from a laser beam," or "You know, don't tell anyone this, but there were UFOs seen in this very spot yesterday, but the government is covering it up because they don't want to cause widespread panic."

STEP THREE—Sit back and feel ashamed over all the trouble that you've started.

ADDENDUM 6-2

SOME LITTLE-KNOWN FACTS ABOUT
THE TRAVIS WALTON UFO ABDUCTION CASE

The 1975 Travis Walton UFO abduction case is considered one of the most famous and impressive of all such cases. The *National Enquirer* declared it the most impressive UFO case of the year and awarded Travis $100,000. It has become a staple incident in UFO literature and is one of the key alien abduction cases in the canon. It formed the basis for a feature film entitled *Fire in the Sky*. [6]

- Two weeks before the alleged abduction, NBC had aired a "true life" prime time made-for-TV movie entitled "The UFO Incident." The movie dramatized the even more famous abduction of Betty and Barney Hill.
- During the five days in which Travis Walton was missing, his family expressed very little concern for his well-being. In fact, during a 65-minute tape-recorded interview with Fred Sylavanus of the organization Ground Saucer Watch (not a skeptics group), Duane Walton, Travis's older brother, never once expressed concern for his younger brother's safety, although he did speculate that Travis might be "on his way to the UFOnaut's home planet to be dissected like a frog or stuffed and put in a museum." [7]
- Shortly before the incident, Travis told his mother that if he was ever abducted by a UFO, then she shouldn't worry as he would be returned safe and sound.

- At the urging of the *National Enquirer*, Travis was given a poly-graph test. When the polygraph operator concluded that Travis was being deceitful, the *Enquirer* attempted to get him to sign a document swearing him to secrecy. They then followed up this first test with a second by a different tester, which concluded that Travis was not being deceitful. [8]
- Travis Walton had been found guilty of forgery and burglary in the past.
- Travis and his family had a reputation among several of their neighbors for pulling pranks and hoaxes of various sorts.
- Duane and Travis Walton, as well as many of their friends and family, were avid fans of UFO literature and believed in them wholeheartedly. Most experienced UFO investigators consider reports by nonenthusiasts more reliable than those by such rabid believers. Duane and Travis and their family all believed that UFO abductions occurred regularly and frequently discussed how they would behave if given the opportunity to be abducted by a UFO or to ride in a flying saucer.
- At the time of the abduction, Travis and Duane Walton were involved in a logging contract with the United States Forest Service. They were way behind in their work and if they did not finish on schedule or find a way out of their contractual obligations, then they would be penal-ized financially and have difficulty getting similar contracts in the future. The contract, like most such contracts, included an "acts of God" clause. This catch-all clause meant that if the loggers were unable to finish due to unforeseeable circumstances, then they would be released from their contractual obligations without penalty. Although this clause was intended to provide for the possibility of things such as terrible weather, natural disasters, and forest fires dis-rupting the loggers and preventing completion of the work, a genuine UFO abduction causing the loss of one worker and forcing the others to cease operations to go look for him would definitely count.

Could the Travis Walton UFO abduction case have been a hoax? Clearly the possibility must be considered, as we can see a pattern of deceit, a motive, and the ability to carry out such a hoax. Decide for yourself.

ADDENDUM 6-3

OUTLINES FOR CROP CIRCLE HOAXING

1) Knock down grass or crops.
2) Do so in a pattern.
3) Make it magnetic.
4) Make it radioactive.
5) Don't get caught.

ENDNOTES

1   For those who are interested, the title page of the report reads, "Operation Animal Mutilation–Report of the District Attorney, First Judicial District, State of New Mexico, by Kenneth M. Rommel, Jr., Project Director, June 1980.

2   Most people who have studied such things feel that most individuals who claim to have been abducted by UFOs are sincere. This does not, however, mean that they have necessarily been abducted. Skeptical investigators have argued that they seem to be misinterpreting some common benign sleep disorders known as "sleep paralysis" and "hypnopompic hallucinations." In the bulk of such cases, the actual memories of these experiences have been distorted and changed by the clumsy misuse of hypnosis. For further examples, one can read *UFO Abductions: A Dangerous Game* by Phillip J. Klass or *They Call It Hypnosis* or *Hidden Memories*, both by Robert Baker, a psychologist who has studied such phenomena extensively.

    I also have written about it. See the bibliography.

3   Actually, this isn't quite true. There is at least one company out there that sells UFO abduction insurance. If you are abducted by a UFO and the company feels that your claim is believable, then they will pay you $1 million at the rate of one dollar a year. See, all it takes is some imagination and lateral thinking and there's always a way to make a buck with these things.

4   Believe it or not, despite the fact that UFO abduction experiences can be explained by more conventional means, a very small percentage of psychotherapists have come to believe that aliens really are abducting human beings. The bulk of these psychotherapists have come under fire from their profession or, in some cases, the universities where they teach.

It should be pointed out that the more I learn about psychotherapy, the more scared I get. For a complete exposé of the problem and a guide to choosing a competent psychotherapist, I highly recommend *Beware the Talking Cure* by Terrence Campbell, 1994, Upton Books, Boca Raton, FL.

5   For what it's worth, down in Peru and nearby parts of South America, there are these really funky lines and shapes called the Nazca lines. Nobody knows why the Indians made them, as they can only be seen from above. Religious purposes is the prime suspected motive.

For centuries, people have been speculating as to how the lines were created. These speculations probably reached their strangest peak when Eric Von Daniken wrote a series of books in which he claimed space aliens were responsible and directed the process from spaceships.

6   I finally sat down and watched this one. It was kind of mediocre, and *The Fortean Times* claims that they had updated aspects of the story in order to make it conform to the current view of UFO abductions.

7   Klass, *UFO Abductions*, p. 26.

8   This incident says a lot not only about the Travis Walton case and the standards of the *National Enquirer* but the reliability of polygraph machines when used as lie detectors.

Suburban Mysticism in 12 Easy Steps!

The Not Quite So New Age

"But your thinking is old. The world is changing. Surely you must be open to change. A New Age is coming, an era when much of these things which you mock will be accepted and understood by all."

"Maybe," said the guru, munching on a wing.

"Shall you continue with your mocking when that day arrives?"

"Maybe."

"When the great New Age arrives, then surely you shall regret your words . . ."

WHERE WILL YOU GO AFTER DEATH?

* Why you may feel the comforting presence of lost loved ones during their funerals (p. 15)

* Do you have a guardian angel—some people have more than one! (p. 110)

* Who meets you right-after death? (p. 27)

* Who serves as your most severe critic at the end of your life — it's not who you might think! (p. 51)

* What happens to souls who caused extreme suffering to others in life? (p. 48)

* Who is in your "soul group" — your inner circle of significant souls united for eternity! (p. 88)

* The explanation for homosexuality (p. 66)

* Why all souls have the opportunity to participate in creation of lower forms of intelligent life (p. 188)

* How to change your karma! (p. 51)

* Why some souls choose life in a damaged body (p. 222)

* The mark of an advanced soul (p. 248)

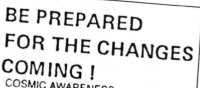

BE PREPARED FOR THE CHANGES COMING !

COSMIC AWARENESS, the Universal Mind, explains UFOs, the Alien Presence, Bigfoot, etc., plus spiritual philosophy, life-after-death. Sample newsletter free!

Why are you here on Earth...? Where will you go after death...? What will happen when you get there...?

While many books have been written about past lives and the near-death experience, little has been published that offers scientific proof of the **ongoing existence** of our souls as we await rebirth — UNTIL NOW! Finally, the time has come for mankind to know the truth about the Spirit World.

Here in the good old U.S. of A., one of my all-time favorite countries, there exists something that's kind of sort of known as the "New Age" movement. Being a trendy sort of movement, it is currently looking for a new name, having tired of the old one. Some candidates seem to be "the Metaphysical Interests," "Holistic Spirituality," and "Spiritualistic Sciences," among others. As New Agers refuse to consider my two favorite candidates, "the Even Newer Age Movement" and the "Whole Body and Soul, Inner Being, Spiritual Bowel Movement," I will not consider any of theirs and will in turn, stubbornly and antagonistically, refer to it as the New Age movement. [1]

The New Age movement is, and always has been, kind of a strange, eclectic place. There is no real New Age ideology in the conventional sense. Instead, the New Age is more of an *approach* to life than anything else.

What typifies New Agers is their attempt to live life as an experiential process, with a strong emphasis on self-growth and exploring spiritual paths. In this, I agree with the movement and respect its goals. The problem arises when one examines the ways in which New Agers seek, evaluate, and decide which paths they wish to follow and which practices they wish to adhere to. The New Age scene is extremely varied, yet its many esoteric beliefs often contradict one another, both in theory and practice. Although it would seem that choices must be made, most New Agers, as will be explained later, sidestep this dilemma neatly.

Many New Age devotees are dissatisfied with the conventional lifestyle and values that our society has traditionally stressed, finding them dull, flat, and meaningless. They have little respect for traditional religions (at least those of white people) and scientific theories, feeling both to be materialistic, constricting, and dissatisfying. (I strongly suspect that many New Agers have some unresolved anger toward their parents and the religion they were raised in, if any.)

Unfortunately, once one discounts religion and science, you have pretty much discredited logic, traditional morality, and societal and interpersonal obligations as the basis for making decisions. What you are left with is primarily a rather hedonistic, relativistic, fluid, and ever-changing environment where major lifestyle changes are made on the basis of faddish trends, temporary cycles, and bizarre group delusions and then confirmed with hunches, impulses, and strange emotions. Research is usually done with a variety of divination and fortune-telling methods. [2]

Many New Agers go so far as to reject not just reality but the entire concept of reality altogether. Their oft-repeated claim is that the world as we see it exists only in our minds. Therefore, we create our own reality. Although a philosopher or a psychologist would

129

see some validity in this statement, to many New Agers the idea is taken far beyond anything reasonable. "I'm God! You're God! We're all God!" is the mantra of such people. Nevertheless, having come to this view, outside confirmation of an idea is discredited because what is true for one person is seen as not necessarily true for another. Emotions and delusions rule. Common sense, logic, and careful observation are thrown out the window. Devotees generally see nothing wrong with this and instead encourage each other to explore new paths and seek to respect each other's choices as much as possible.

Surprisingly, many New Agers have, through one means or another (generally via husbands, parents, and other poorly evolved people with jobs), a relatively large amount of income to spend on pursuing "self-actualization." The environment simply is amazingly ripe for those who wish to perpetrate fraud. Such frauds can range from the quite small up to the very large.

On the small end, we have the following example. Many New Agers believe, for reasons firmly based in delusion, that crystals such as quartz hold magical powers. The idea is espoused that, through using crystals to focus one's psychic powers, healing can be accomplished and bad luck banished. Naturally, the widely available crystals fetch different prices based on such factors as their mineral content, color, clarity, luster, size, and shape. [3]

Recently, one New Age store I visited was selling "special" crystals for an extra high price. Why were they special? Well, they had red streaks in them, but more importantly, according to the vendor these crystals were used as energy batteries by the ancient Atlanteans before their civilization sank under the sea, hence the extra high price the vendor was asking! [4]

I asked my new acquaintance how this knowledge came to be known. After all, even if Atlantis did exist, nobody knows where it was, much less what sort of crystals, if any, the people who lived there happened to use to focus their psychic energies. [5] Perhaps, I thought, a 9,000-year-old Atlantean had been discovered somewhere in the Pacific Ocean having used such a crystal to help him tread

Lift the veil between this world and the world of *All Knowledge* — when you possess the secret of the Crystal Vibration!

Did you know that spiritual guides, angels and devas are *waiting* to work with you? But they can't assist you until you know the *secret* of vibrational energy!

Why? Because when you know how to use vibrational energy, **it is like having a direct phone line to** th...

easy to obtain and **amazingly easy to use**. To play its sacred music, simply tap a wand on the side of the bowl to create a bell-like sound, or rotate the wand around the outside or inside of the bowl. You will unleash a **spiral of energy** that resonates with the limitless dimensions of the Divine.

The wisdom of the ancients unites with the wonders of high technology to help you to:

- Develop clairvoyance
- **Attune to spirit guides, angels and devas**
- Astrally project
- **Perform long-distance healing**
- Balance the hemispheres of your brain
- **Induce altered states of consciousness**
- Project energy through your hands
- **Cleanse your auric field**
- Create a sacred spiral of energy
- **Manifest prayers and affirmations**
- Purify and cleanse water
- **Commune with your inner essence**
- Intensify meditations
- **Rid yourself of toxins, negativities and harmful energy patterns**

water for millennia. But no, this was not the case. The information, I was told by the vendor, *had been channeled!*

Now channeling itself is quite a strange thing that has a great potential for fraud and bears describing in full. In many cases it is a fine example of a large New Age fraud.

In many cultures, there exists a belief that under certain circumstances, spirits of animals, deities, or the dead can enter the body of a living human and speak with his or her voice. [6] New Agers, following their maxim "if mom and dad did it, it's probably bad; if somebody foreign and exotic did it, it's probably good!" have picked up the practice, traditionally known as shamanism or spirit mediumship, but renamed it channeling. (This is not to be confused with channel surfing, which is another nineties sort of way to spend one's leisure time.)

Fraudulent channeling is relatively easy, and a good channeler can make pretty good money. You simply pretend to do it. In fact, there is virtually no way to distinguish a "real" channeler from a "false" channeler. Even in countries where such practices are traditionally done as part of the popular religion and have been practiced over the centuries, it is difficult for both the priests and the laypeople to distinguish when the medium is truly speaking with the voice of a deity. [7] Few New Agers try very hard to do so anyway. Nevertheless, one good test, almost universally followed, is whether the channeler is saying what the believers wish to hear and would expect a God to say.

Although practice doesn't hurt, it really doesn't take skill to be a channeler once you learn the sort of performance that the audience expects. In fact, it has been said that channeling is really nothing more than "bad ventriloquism" [8] My own observations of channeling bear this out. In some cases, you can convince an audience that you are channeling simply by rolling your eyes back and mumbling ever so slightly.

Of course, if you are going to channel, then you will need a spirit, a higher being, a really dead guy from long ago, or some other allegedly superior entity to pretend to channel. Although in traditional cultures this choice is limited, we, with our modern convenience-oriented civilization, can channel virtually anyone or anything we want to!

Among the entities actively being channeled today are a number of benevolent angels. Angels are cool. Angels are hip. Angels may be ancient, but they are still very nineties!

Channelers also bless us with a variety of space aliens anxious to share their transgalactic wisdom with us. Remember, space aliens may be funny looking, but this isn't their fault. They are still our friends. (But then again, would you really want your sister to marry one?)

From time to time dead people are channeled. In today's society, however, these are not particularly popular. I suspect the audience tends to find them comparatively boring, and few New Agers have a strong interest in history. Besides, dead people can have their existence or lifestyle verified. It cannot be entirely coincidental that the bulk of the dead guys channeled come from such places as Atlantis, Mu, and other civilizations considered to be imaginary. [9]

Although dolphins are beautiful animals, to many they are much, much more. Dolphins have taken on a symbolic significance in the New Age movement, being seen as a peaceful, contented, highly evolved and enlightened race of beings who live in harmony with their environment in a way that humans do not. Some claim that dolphins have the perfect society and may even be the descendants of de-evolved Atlanteans who returned to the sea after finding life on land too difficult! [10] Placed in this context, can it be the least bit surprising that dolphin spirits are occasionally channeled by us poorly evolved land-dwelling mammals? In some cases, the dolphin-spirit doesn't even need its speech translated into English but can simply squeak out its message in high-pitched dolphin warbles. (Among the rumored pearls of wisdom are, "Give me a fish!")

Deities are, of course, popular, and some channelers claim to be speaking with the voice of Jesus. Of course, it's Jesus with a very strange twist, but it's marketed as the same 2,000-year-old dead Jewish guy. Various Buddhas such as Kuan Yin and the Matireya Buddha have made appearances as well.

Other channelers purport to speak with the spirit of a "universal intelligence." A universal intelligence is basically just like a deity but without producing those nasty "but I am beyond religion" knee-jerk reactions that New Agers hate so much.

When creating entities to channel, do not hesitate to use your imagination. If you find yourself lacking in imagination, do not hes-

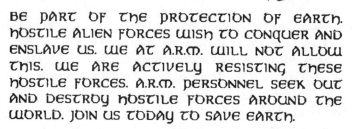

ALIEN RESISTANCE MOVEMENT
"FIGHTING FOR THE UNIVERSE"

BE PART OF THE PROTECTION OF EARTH.
HOSTILE ALIEN FORCES WISH TO CONQUER AND
ENSLAVE US. WE AT A.R.M. WILL NOT ALLOW
THIS. WE ARE ACTIVELY RESISTING THESE
HOSTILE FORCES. A.R.M. PERSONNEL SEEK OUT
AND DESTROY HOSTILE FORCES AROUND THE
WORLD. JOIN US TODAY TO SAVE EARTH.

RESEARCHERS AND SUPPLIERS OF ADVANCED
TECHNOLOGY TO DESTROY ALIENS AND
PROTECT EARTH. THESE INCLUDE•PSIONIC
PISTOLS•PSYCHIC PROTECTION FIELD
INCREASERS•ALIEN LASER WEAPONS•FUTURE
ARMAMENTS BOOKS, COURSES AND TRAINING FOR
ALIEN FIGHTERS•TIME TRAVEL DEVICES
•PROTECTIVE WATERS •IMPLANT
REMOVALS•FULL BODY HEALING•SONIC SOUND
WEAPONS & MORE!! **SEND $4.00 FOR COMPLETE**

itate to seek out an expert source, such as a junior high comic book collector, to assist you with ideas.

If you need an example, here's my favorite channeling incident. Until recently, there was one person on the West Coast who channeled the spirit of Barbie, the 12-inch tall, plastic, blond-haired, large-busted, anorexic fashion doll that half the girls in America grew up with. Apparently, Barbie's first channeled words were, "I need respect." Unfortunately, for those of us who yearned for the self-described "stereotypical wisdom of the 60s and 70s" from the "archetypal feminine plastic essence," the Mattel toy corporation took a dim view of Barbie's striking out on her own and struck back with the threat of a multimillion dollar lawsuit, effectively quashing the wisdom of the ages and silencing the channeler. Barbie, it seems, still gets no respect. [11]

Channeling is popular. Channeled books, tapes, and more are available in bookstores across America. So far, there really doesn't seem to be much skill or imagination involved in the frauds described. In fact, those mentioned are based not so much on cleverness and imagination as on audacity.

Still, here are some points to remember. First of all, believe it or not, when you channel an entity, make sure that you remember to copyright it, just as famed channeler J.Z. Knight did with her famous entity, Ramtha. [12] This will help prevent those bizarre lawsuits that have actually happened when one person decided to channel another's entity without the first person's permission.

There are certain protocols that are normally adhered to, but they are quite simple. For example, it is the custom for a channeler to later feign ignorance of anything said while channeling. A few facial grimaces prior to the act help. Just a few, though. Unlike most cultures, where a shaman must actively work to enter a trance, in ours mediumship has become like everything else—instant!

While in channeling mode, a scam artist can pull an additional fast one if so inclined. The above-mentioned J.Z. Knight has come under fire when Ramtha recommended to her clients that they purchase Arabian horses. Coincidentally, it just so happens that J.Z. Knight raises Arabian horses. [13] Peculiar advice on which real estate purchases will benefit listeners following predicted earth-shaking cataclysms of all sorts has also occurred.

I attended one channeling session, where much to my surprise the channeler's assistants didn't seem to fit my notions of what a New Ager should look like. I mean, these guys looked downright normal! You know, like the sort of guys who'd be more likely to plop themselves in front of the boob tube with a six pack and some chips and catch the game on a Saturday afternoon, not the sort who you'd expect to see facilitating the cross-dimensional channeling of a higher being. I confess, I was much less surprised when I observed them hanging out after the session and striking up conversations with the babes who had attended.

As disturbing as such scenes can be, they simply have to be

expected in the New Age scene. The thing is, New Age people fool themselves so much and so badly already that there's very little left for a con man to do to take advantage of them! By rejecting logic and choosing to act on impulse, they frequently take all the work out of it.

The late Randall N. Baer gave this example in his work, *Inside the New Age Nightmare*:

"Some schools of New Age bodywork feel that psychological traumas also are lodged in deep muscle tissues. Therefore to release these traumas and restore body harmony, it becomes necessary for the practitioner to grind fists, fingers, elbows, and knees deeply into virtually every major muscle group in the body of the hapless recipient.

"This is severely excruciating to say the least. The howls, shrieks, and murderous screams that would fill the air eventually became 'normal,' though during the first few weeks the place sounded at times like a torture chamber.

"Then it was *my turn* . . .

"Sometimes a couple of assistants were required to hold me down while the practitioner tried to make my calf muscles 'one with the table' via extreme elbow pressure. This is a series of treatments profoundly etched in my memory." [14]

Sadly, Mr. Baer doesn't answer one of the key questions that I have. Just how much, exactly, per day, was he paying for the privilege of being held down and beaten on with elbows? But he does tell us many other fascinating things. For example, on another retreat:

"One practice was to get up in the morning and quickly drink an entire gallon of heavily salted water. Why? So you immediately could regurgitate it all back out . . . if you can imagine a bathroom of people doing this at the same time, it's certainly a fine way to start the morning." [15]

Many otherwise obvious scams can be made to succeed by simply reworking them with a New Age twist. For an example, let's look at a disturbing fad that broke out in the San Francisco Bay area in 1987. This scheme, known as the "Airplane Game," attracted a large number of people, all of whom invested $1,500 apiece in what was obviously a pyramid scheme.

Pyramid schemes are one of the oldest, shadiest deals around and for this reason are generally illegal. In a pyramid scheme, each participant contributes money. They are generally obligated to recruit others. The recruits contribute money, and this money is then split up among those already in the scheme. Each person in the scheme benefits and receives a considerable profit from their investment just so long as the number of recruits keeps growing.

Of course, continuous recruitment and growth is impossible. The mathematics of the operation simply dictate that eventually the number of people and the amount of money available for the scheme will run out, so ultimately the profits slow down and finally stop coming in altogether.

One example of a common pyramid scheme is the chain letter. I have been involved in a couple of these over the years, but I have never received anything from a single one. Sometimes, of course, you can make a lot of money on a pyramid scheme, but only if you start at the top. Any way you look at it, the mathematics dictate that a considerable number of people will lose their investment.

In the Airplane Game, participants were expected to contribute $1,500 apiece for the privilege of buying a "seat" as a "passenger" on the "airplane." And passenger was the lowest level in the four-tiered system of ranks. Above it there was "flight attendant," "co-pilot," and "pilot." When a passenger recruited two other people who wished to buy a seat, then he would move up to the flight attendant

ANDREIKA

I WILL CAST A SPELL FOR YOU!

I can cast a spell to make one love another, or cause a person to change his mind about a relationship, or bring two people together.

My magical powers are beyond your imagination. I can cast a spell in your behalf regarding a relationship, your financial situation, future events, or whatever is important to you. I have the

rank. The pilot would then leave the game, collecting the entry fees of the eight passengers at this time. This would come to $12,000, and it was seen as his reward for having worked his way up the ranks.

To anyone with a passing knowledge of mathematics, the Airplane Game was destined to crash. Yet the passengers minds weren't on mathematics. Instead, their thoughts were focused on enlightenment.

The Airplane Game was billed as a "learning experience." Participants were told that by playing they would "revitalize their experience with money" and learn the process of "generating abundance." The participants held weekly meetings, at which they discussed their progress and what they had learned. While attending these meetings, New Agey sounding pseudonyms were used. Some examples were Laughing Buddha, Star Child, Icarus, and Blue Pearl, among others. At one such meeting, a "feminist shaman" was invited to make the rounds of the room pounding a drum and blessing everyone with a "prosperity chant."

Although pyramid schemes are illegal, the local police gave the Airplane Game a very low priority. Participants were, they reasoned, eager, anxious, and knowingly entering a get-rich scheme that was transparently doomed to failure. Although there was some talk of arresting some of those involved, other crimes and frauds always

138

seemed to have a higher priority. Local newspapers sought to expose the scheme as immoral, illegal, and just plain stupid, yet those involved were seemingly beyond help.

Ultimately, the inevitable happened and recruits became harder and harder to find. When it became obvious that many participants were not going to "pilot out" and receive their $12,000, recruiting became virtually impossible. As many of the participants involved realized that a "seat on the airplane" was not an opportunity but a trap, they naturally became less eager to sell seats to their friends. The project fizzled out and died.

Many were disappointed and felt that they had been scammed. Others felt that the process had been sabotaged by some sort of supernatural force. One participant reasoned that the project had come to a halt due to a "conditioned prejudice" against receiving money among the members. To overcome this prejudice, and to try and open people's minds, he passed out handfuls of "prosperity quarters."

Others, strangely, sought to make the best of the situation and claimed that they had, in fact, learned a lot in their workshop. Some players pointed to various intangible lessons that they had learned about money. Others realized that if they could recruit people to contribute money and time to an unworkable pyramid scheme, then it should be possible to recruit the same level of investment and commitment to other, more worthwhile and beneficial projects. Some even went so far as to feel that the experience and its intangible benefits had been well worth the $1,500 fee. [16]

To a thinking person, the New Age movement is a disturbing tragedy waiting to happen. The varieties of New Age scams could go on forever. Perhaps they will. We can only hope not.

For the present, however, it seems that the New Age movement or some sort of renamed equivalent is going to be a part of our society for the conceivable future. People, it seems, need a place where they can experiment with new ways to find meaning in their lives. Furthermore, few can deny that there will always be people who will wish to study practices and arts that cannot be proven or, in some

connections

communications potential

This group was founded in 1981 and through these many years a group of beings, who refer to themselves as Leians, has channeled through

There are four entities who have participated with us from their group but the two who are most active are called KA-LI and VA-LLUM; pronounced kay-lee and vlumm respectively.

KA-LI contacted for the first time when

roaming around. They do believe that all life forms change state as an evolutionary process through spiritual awareness.

The last of the four entities is part of a group called "WATCHERS". It is known and accepted that WATCHERS generally do not interact with other life forms. They only observe, hence the name WATCHERS. We have been fortunate to speak with one known as RHA.

cases, have been disproven long ago. This book cannot change that.

Nevertheless, let me just end with a final plea to all those involved in the New Age movement:

Wake up!!

As I write, I have in my hand the program for "The Whole Planet Exposition" held in June 1996 in Santa Fe, New Mexico. Among the workshops offered—and I'm not making this up—were the following:

- Meet Your Guardian Angel
- How to Talk to Animals
- The Human Voice as a Healing Instrument
- Nostradamus: Prophecies for the Next Twenty Years
- Talking With the Dead
- Discovering Your Past Lives and Other Dimensions
- The Philadelphia Experiment: New Developments in Time Travel
- Mother Earth is Becoming the Heart Center of Our Solar System and Galaxy
- Healing Through Spiritual Surgery
- The Universal Interconnection of Star Children: Information from the 7th Through 12th Dimensions

Hello everybody! Message from Earth here! These things are really silly! Somebody is making them up!

140

But then again, why knock it? As a friend of mine once said, "I used to go to Star Trek conventions. Now I go to New Age gatherings. The women are better looking, and they're really friendly if you pretend to take this stuff seriously."

ADDENDUM 7-1

SOME IMPORTANT NEW AGE BUZZWORDS

Check out this list. Pick a favorite or two. Learn as many as you can. Then sprinkle your speech liberally with them. You will be amazed at how quickly you will have New Age believers eating out of your hand, firmly convinced that you are one of them.

A Step Closer to Higher
  Consciousness
Awakening
Casting Out Negativity
Consciousness
Consciousness Raising
Energizing
Energy
Enlightening
Exercise
Experiential
Experiential Process
Higher Consciousness
Holistic
Holographic
Human Potential
Increasing Spiritual Awareness
Karmic

Liberating
Networking
Oneness
Personal Growth
Personal Transformations
Positive
Positivity
Removing Ingrained
  Prejudices
Spiritually Awakening
Spiritually Uplifting
Synergistic
Therapeutic
Transformational
Trust Building
Unity
Unshackling Ingrained
  Prejudices

If you wish to talk a New Ager into doing something, you can't just say, "Hey buddy, loan me some money." You will have much more success if you say, "Excuse me, I couldn't help sharing my thought with you that it would be a spiritually uplifting, transformational experience if we were to share in a financial encounter experience by you loaning me some money. Although I know that you may not feel quite ready for the experience, and I can empathize with that, I really sense that this would help you overcome some of your ingrained prejudices about material wealth and objective reality. I think we would both find such a process to be spiritually enlightening, karmically uplifting, and a great transformational opportunity."

Whatever you do, avoid the terms "groovy" and "grok" (as in "I can grok what you are saying.") These are passé. It is, however, acceptable to make references to experiences that you have "had" or "shared" in a past life in Atlantis or elsewhere.

ENDNOTES

1   This is a little like referring to your Born-Again Christian acquaintances as "religious." They will correct you, and they will resent it, but, seeing as you're right and they're wrong and everybody knows it, who really cares?

2   I am not making this up. Believe me, it is absolutely disturbing to watch the way some of these people make decisions regarding the important issues in their lives. A joke's a joke, but think hard before you go around playing games with New Age believers. They *will* believe you!

3   One of the great ironies of the New Age movement is that a surprising amount of these "holistic" crystals are strip-mined in an environmentally unsound manner.

4   What's scary is that he may have believed this himself, in which case the wholesaler or somebody higher up had discovered this marketing ploy.

5   There are literally thousands of books available on Atlantis, and it is my impression that virtually every single one of them contradicts all of the rest in

practically all claims as to where Atlantis was and what it may have been like there, if it indeed existed. One I like is DeCamp's *Lost Continents*, which, by the way, does not mention crystals once.

6   Once again, there are many good works that provide an introduction to this fascinating subject. One classic in the field is Mircea Eliade's *Shamanism: Archaic Techniques of Ecstasy.*

7   At this point, I'd just like to make it clear that I do not believe all "spirit mediums" to be conscious frauds, although I do discount the belief that the supernatural is involved. It is my opinion that there are some very interesting psychological things going on, including altered states of consciousness on the part of those mediums who really do believe themselves to be "possessed."

8   This description of channeling was originally made by Jamy Ian Swiss, a professional magician.

9   Not only is it less exciting, but channeling historical figures poses a risk of making errors in speech or factual details. For a time, a woman channeled an entity known as "Michael." Michael claimed to be the deceased spirit of a blind sixteenth-century Scottish fiddle player and spoke with a thick brogue. Sarah Grey Thomson, a professor of linguistics who enjoys investigating paranormal claims, became interested in Michael's speech patterns. In her article "Entities in the Linguistic Minefield" in the Summer 1989 issue of *Skeptical Inquirer*, she explains how Michael's speech patterns are completely unlike those of a genuine Scotsman of the period, even one trying to speak like a twentieth-century American. In fact, his speech bore a much stronger resemblance to a movie Scotsman than anything else.

10   But who can blame them? I mean, if most people had the choice between working for a living or floating around in the ocean all day with nothing to do but eat fish, fuck, and stay out of tuna cans, which would they choose?

11   I am not making this up! See the *Fortean Times*, number 68, p. 7, and number 78, page 7 once again.

12   See the essay, "Isness Is Her Business: Shirley MacLaine," by Martin Gardner in *Not Necessarily the New Age* (Prometheus Books, 1988).

13   Ibid., p. 193.

14   Baer, p. 17. It should be noted that Baer's book details his change from becoming a New Age enthusiast to an evangelical Christian. Nevertheless, regardless of your views, this work includes a lot of very informative inside stuff on the New Age movement.

15   Baer, p. 16.

16   Details of the Airplane Game come from "The Airplane Game: Inside a New Age Pyramid Scheme" by Jeff Greenwald, which was published in *The Fringes of Reason: A Whole Earth Catalog*, pp. 35–42.

Hi! I'm Pete! Fly Me!

8

Meditation Tricks

"You stink," cried the pilgrim.
"Oh well, I'll teach you something anyway. First, we must meditate . . ."

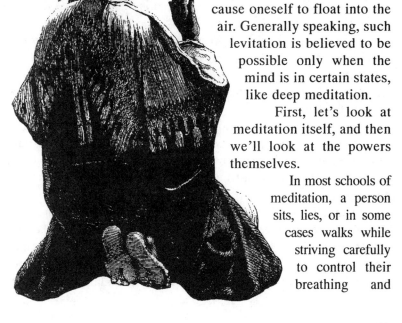

Out on the fringes of reality, there lies a belief that the mind has untapped mystical powers. These include supernatural control of the body and even the ability to cause oneself to float into the air. Generally speaking, such levitation is believed to be possible only when the mind is in certain states, like deep meditation.

First, let's look at meditation itself, and then we'll look at the powers themselves.

In most schools of meditation, a person sits, lies, or in some cases walks while striving carefully to control their breathing and their thoughts. The intention of this is usually to relax the person, improve control over their mind and their emotions, and to enter a "meditative state." A meditative state is an "altered state of consciousness" where the person feels different than they normally do because of some action of the brain. There are a wide variety of altered states of consciousness (many of my favorites having to do with beer). [1]

While in a meditative state, the person generally feels relaxed, peaceful, detached, and somewhat mystical. Many find this state desirable and spend time meditating regularly. Others criticize meditation, generally feeling that there are other equally effective ways to relax without indulging in something they find distastefully esoteric and otherworldly. Despite this, I find meditation a valid activity and engage in it from time to time myself.

STOPPING YOUR HEARTBEAT

One point that the critics and myself can agree on, however, is that there are a lot of exaggerated claims out there regarding the effectiveness of meditation. Among these is the belief that through meditation a person can stop his heartbeat completely. The truth is that when a person is relaxed, both his heartbeat and respiratory rate slow down. As meditation produces a relaxed state, it follows logically that meditation does, in fact, slow the heartbeat. As for the limit on this cardiac slowing, this is uncertain, and much careful study waits to be done.

The issue is further complicated by the possibility of fakery having been done throughout the ages. Although periodic reports have surfaced of mystics who could stop their heart completely, this does not necessarily mean that the phenomenon has occurred.

If you'd like to demonstrate the ability to alter or halt your heartbeat, there are two possible courses of action open to you. The first is that you can search really hard, find a real mystic, and convince him to take you on as a student. This will take years of practice, not to mention a real mystic, and you run the quite high risk of meeting up with a fraud and wasting a great deal of time, money, and emotional energy.

The second is that you can use fakery. To do this, place a small ball, such as a golf ball, over your brachial artery on the inside of your upper arm. At this point on your body a large artery runs close to the bone. With a little bit of gentle pressure to this point, it is possible to reduce or temporarily cut off the flow of blood to the wrist and, more importantly, the point on the wrist where most people check for a pulse.

Naturally, you don't want to do this for hours at a stretch, as it is unhealthy. If you feel your arm falling asleep, remember that this is your body's way of saying, "Hey bozo! Enough of the stupid tricks. Cut it out or you will hurt yourself!" [2]

LEVITATION

Another example of a claimed "untapped human mind power" is the idea that meditation can produce levitation. In theory, it is difficult to see how the idea could work. The physics required to explain such a thing require that either a force be applied to lift up the body or else the effects of gravity be cut off altogether. In the first case, we would have to identify the source of the power. Is it, whatever it might be, pushing or pulling? Why isn't it creating heat or pressure under the levitator? If it is pulling upward instead of pushing downward, then it would still seem to need something to pull up with? If the levitator has lost considerable weight so that their new weight is comparable to that of a large helium balloon or something, then we must ask where did the weight go? If it is the second case, and gravity is cut off, then physics states that the person should pop upward like a lost helium balloon and strike the ceiling or else float away entirely! Furthermore, when one sees photos of levitating meditators, why doesn't their hair float up instead of just hanging down next to their body? [3]

Nevertheless, the claims continue, and there are piles and piles of evidence behind them, yet all of it seems to consist exclusively of still photographs. The promoters of such ideas release large quantities of these, yet they refuse to provide videotapes or allow nonbelieving witnesses to observe the phenomenon. Why? Go figure! I admit ignorance, but then again, all concerned will admit that I am not particularly enlightened.

Faced with such circumstances, it seems that all a guy can do is ponder at the mystical workings of the universe and then simply make his own levitation photos. There are some simple ways to do this.

The traditional method of hoaxing a levitation photo is to get someone to jump up into the air and then snap a photo. The picture must be taken at very high speed, preferably using a strobe flash, in order to avoid any telltale blurring of the finished product.

When attempting to take these photos, however, I soon ran into a problem. Traditionally, in most schools of meditation that claim the power of levitation, the student is shown levitating in mid-air while sitting in a cross-legged position. It is believed by skeptics that they actually jump up into the air from this position. This is no mean feat, and few can do it. In fact, in most of these schools of meditation, the ability to levitate is seen as the end product of a long series of steps. For example, in the first step the student meditates and creates a "feeling of lightness" in his body. In the second step, the student begins to bounce a little bit. In the third step, the student actually jumps into the air and believes himself to float for a second or two in mid-air longer than gravity would normally dictate. And so on.

In short, these people are trained to hop up and down from a squat-legged position. You are not! Now that's not to say that you can't do it, but it's tricky, and it's much more difficult than it sounds. Although a trained gymnast with a trampoline might find it simple, clumsy free-lance writers who spend too much time sitting on their butt find it hard to gain any height.

A second option, which I seriously considered, is to hurl oneself off a reasonable height in a squat-legged position. Then, while engaged in a downward motion, snap the photo. The catch here is—you guessed it—landing! Keep in mind the "no permanent damage" rule of stupid tricks. If you must come crashing to the ground, ensure that you have a soft padding or large pool of water or something similar to prevent injury. Remember, it's tough to explain away the cast if you injure yourself doing something like this.

Of course, as shown in Addendum 8-1, it's not necessary to have these photos taken from a squatting position, but then again, it does help produce the overall desired effect.

ADDENDUM 8-1

VARIOUS METHODS FOR HOAXING
LEVITATION PHOTOS

METHOD ONE: TAKE A PHOTO OF THE PERSON
WHILE IN MID-BOUNCE

The traditional method of hoaxing a levitation photo is to get someone to jump up into the air and then snap a photo. The picture must be taken at very high speed, preferably using a strobe flash, in order to avoid any blurring of the finished product.

METHOD TWO: MAKE THE FLOOR
LOOK LIKE A WALL

If you are clumsy, like my assistants and I tend to be, and find it difficult to jump up and down from a squatting position, then you may want to try this method instead. First, you acquire some construction materials, create something that looks like a wall, and then lay it flat on the ground. Lie back on it and then snap some photos. You may wish to use an airbrush or other technique to create an artificial shadow under your model.

METHOD THREE: THE DIVING BOARD TECHNIQUE

One of the simplest methods of producing this effect is to simply find a prop on which the "levitator" can sit and then take a picture of him from such an angle that the prop will be concealed in the finished product.

METHOD FOUR: DARK ROOM TECHNIQUES

One of the standard ways to create a levitation photo is to use trick photography. Undoubtedly, computer techniques for altering photos, as briefly presented in Chapter Five, could also be used.

ENDNOTES

1   Altered states of consciousness can be a fascinating subject. For more on it, some good works are *The Psychology of Transcendence* by Andrew Neher, the anthology *Altered States of Consciousness* edited by Charles T. Tart, and various works by Ronald K. Siegel. Herbert Benson has written books specifical-

ly on meditation, and in one, *Beyond the Relaxation Response*, he tells an amusing story of investigating some levitation claims of Tibetan monks.

2   Three fascinating points about this: A) This is a great way to scare school nurses. B) EMTs and other first aid professionals use this pressure point to help control bleeding on the lower arm. C) Helena Petrovna Blavatsky, the influential nineteenth-century mystic and suspected charlatan, had a curious habit of "falling ill" and developing a weak pulse at extremely convenient times during her later life. Theories, anyone? For the details, see *Madame Blavatsky: Priestess of the Occult* by Gertrude Marvin Williams (Lancer Books, Inc., New York, 1946). This book is often found in libraries.

3   See "Levitation: Some Phantasy and Some Physics," by Warner Clements in *The Skeptical Inquirer*, Vol. 13, No. 3, Spring 1989.

Hey, Like Where'd You Learn All This Shit, Anyway?

Establishing a Credible New Age Background

"Who the heck do you think you are?" cried the irate pilgrim. "What gives you the right to shoot off your mouth as if you were somebody special?"

The guru wiped wing sauce all over his jeans. Then he belched in a most enlightened manner.

"Well, you see, I had this teacher once, and this teacher of mine, well, he said . . ."

In previous chapters, I may have left the casual reader with the impression that I consider the great bulk of New Age enthusiasts to be boneheads. This is absolutely correct. It is possible, I feel, to make money by promising to teach New Agers almost anything. We've already mentioned crystals and channeling. As I write, people are paying hard cash to enroll in courses on how to walk through walls without even requesting a demonstration. It seems they liked the meditation courses so much that they assume this advanced course is useful as well. For years, there was a man traveling the country running seminars on how to live without eating or drinking material substances. He called his group the Breatharians. Unfortunately for him, his credibility took a dive and enrollment dropped (but still did not cease!) when he was caught wolfing down a ham and cheese sandwich shortly before a lecture one day.

Most areas have some sort of little New Age/holistic/alternative newsletter that's generally free to pick up and includes a great many ads for a variety of services and courses.[1] Such papers are generally available at New Age bookstores, health food stores, and other places where granola types tend to congregate.

Check them out and you will quite likely find that there are more flaky things being taught in your area than can be found in a cereal box. In the bulk of these cases, the instructor who organized the seminar made money. This is scary. In other cases, the instructor not only made money, but he had many quite satisfied students who felt that they had benefited greatly from taking his course. None of these students were able to demonstrate the powers and abilities that the instructor had promised them, yet they all recommended the seminar quite highly. And some people ask if I have ever seen anything truly unexplained in the world!

Nevertheless, conducting seminars in foolishness does require a certain level of credentials. Sooner or later someone will ask about your qualifications to teach your subject of choice.[2] Now, if you can do what you promise, or at least fake it with some credibility, then you can simply give eager viewers a demonstration. This will do much to impress all concerned and improve your reputation. If this is not possible, then you must brush off potential detractors with a reasonable excuse. Some valid sounding and frequently used brush-offs are:

- "My powers have left me today. Such awesome abilities as mine do not come whenever I wish."
- "Mercury is retrograde, and thus the stars show that it is a bad time to conduct business."

- "You have such a closed mind. You really must learn to open it more."

- "I do not use my powers for frivolous purposes, especially demonstrations for doubters. After all, I know I can do it."

Nevertheless, some will clamor for credentials. "How," they will ask, "did you ever learn the art of Neanderthal Dream Weaving when the Neanderthals have been extinct for tens of thousands of years?" At this point, you better have an answer prepared. It doesn't need to be good. You could just say that it came to you in a dream and I'm sure you would still get students just so long as you can pull of the self-satisfied, semi-enlightened New Ager persona.

Illustration by Ted Kersten.

Still, to increase enrollment in your seminar, it helps to have a plausible sounding source for your teachings. Although we'll look at alternatives later, the method of choice remains the "wise and all-knowing teacher" ploy. You should create your wise and all-knowing teacher with care. Use your imagination. It's not that anybody's going to actually meet him or her or it. But as you teach your courses and seminars, you should drop in asides about this wonderful person who "shared" so much with you. New Age students will love it. If done right, the all-knowing teacher will have charisma. Students will flock from all over just to hear you speak of the wisdom of a well-imagined teacher. Naturally, you will be the only source for this wisdom.

Scams from the Great Beyond

Before you describe your teacher, take care to envision details. These do not necessarily have to be believable, but they must feel right. Your teacher should have a definite personality—kindly, mysterious, wise. He must impart information in a slow and methodical manner, keeping things interesting, and letting the students find the results of these mysterious processes for themselves.

Above all, teachers must be of an appropriate ethnic background, one that will add to their mythical stature, not detract from it. Tibetans and American Indians work best. [3] Irish/Italian crossbreeds from the suburbs of Newark, New Jersey, usually don't work very well.

Most of the masters of pop mysticism have had a teacher. Carlos Castaneda has a Yaqui Indian shaman named Don Juan. Lynn Andrews has a Cree Indian named Agnes Whistling Elk. Shirley MacLaine has an Andean teacher (probably an Indian) of metaphysical arts named David. All of these teachers have made their students a great deal of money, and yet there's a great deal of evidence that these people just don't exist. People have pointed out flaws, inconsistencies, and cultural and geographical errors in all the works of the pop mystics. Nevertheless, the bizarre fact is they just keep on selling just as well as they ever did. In fact, the books and magazine articles exposing these hoaxes tend to come and go from print quickly, while the real thing keeps on selling at a steady pace. [4]

Helena Petrovna Blavatsky is an intriguing woman who in the

New Additional Events In June

Huna For Miracles
Wednesday June 28, 7:30 - 9 pm $10

Huna is a psycho-religious method of the ancient Hawaiian kahunas or "Keepers of the Secret" in performing their particular kinds of "miracles" or "magic". Some of these miracles were healing the sick, solving personal problems, untangling financial and social difficulties and changing the future. These miracles are rooted in the knowledge of how three levels of consciousness (the "Three Selves" of Huna) function effectively. Come meet your 3 selves and get them working harmoniously to create miracles.

nineteenth century was responsible for introducing a great many of the current New Age concepts to the west for the first time. Although many of these originally came from sources such as Asian religions (particularly Hindu mysticism), spiritualism, Western occultism, or bad early science fiction, she reworked and mixed them together into her own school of teachings known as Theosophy. Theosophy still exists today, and the bulk of its teachings are available in two mammoth works called *Isis Unveiled* and *The Secret Doctrine.*

Although it has been proven convincingly that both of these works have been extensively plagiarized from a wide variety of sources, Blavatsky refused to admit this, sticking instead to her story that she had received the teachings from a mysterious group of teachers known as "The Great White Brotherhood." [5] According to Blavatsky, The Great White Brotherhood lived in Tibet and transmitted the information to her by sending her letters using astral travel. If anyone requested proof that such a thing were possible, she would simply show them the letters! Many found this quite convincing.

Blavatsky was a strong and domineering woman with a brilliant but devious mind whose teachings had a great effect on later metaphysical, occult, and New Age groups. [6] Ultimately, the concept of the Great White Brotherhood (and their mythical headquarters, the Great White Lodge) was picked up by quite a few bizarre occult groups who cited it as the source of their teachings. [7] There are still a surprising number of books on it today.

The will to believe is quite strong. For example, although the current New Age bestseller, *The Celestine Prophecy*, is clearly labeled "New Age Fiction," the publisher has released a variety of support materials for those who wish to practice the teachings of the book.

The Puk-Wud-Jies

An ancient tribe of
forest-dwelling little
people may still be
living in Indiana.

And such things aren't unique. An English gentleman by the name of Cyril Henry Hoskins wrote a whole series of books pretending to be a Tibetan monk with mystical powers by the name of T. Lobsang Rampa. There were about a dozen of these, with each one getting progressively sillier. After the first book, Hoskins was unmasked as a hoaxer by a private detective hired by a group of irate Tibetan studies scholars incensed by his strange claims. This had little effect on the series. Hoskins simply shrugged it off, claimed that although he was not, in fact, a Tibetan monk, a real Tibetan monk had been dictating the books to him telepathically. I got a real kick out of the one where Rampa describes his trip to Venus in the flying saucer, and I am looking forward to reading the one that he claims was dictated to him by his Siamese cat. [8]

By the way, the wise old teacher ploy need not be limited to the New Age field. For instance, one wilderness survival writer claims that as a young boy he was taught his survival skills by an Apache Indian in New Jersey who frequently blindfolded him for days so that he would learn to utilize all of his senses. It could be true, but not only are there few Apaches in New Jersey, there are also very few parents who would let a stranger keep their son blindfolded and alone in the woods for days on end. I don't know. Maybe the kid was just lucky to have such open-minded and understanding folks.

The wise old teacher ploy is pretty common in the field of Asian martial arts too. There is no easier way to improve your reputation as a martial arts teacher, particularly in the suburbs, than to pull off the "master" routine. Now, some would argue that, in order to do this properly, you must be born Asian, but this isn't true. Check out David Carridine, an actor who for years made his living wandering around barefoot and speaking heavy-duty, neo-Chinese, pseudomysticism in stilted English, all of it completely inauthentic! And in any event, it's been proven that the Asians themselves have been exaggerating the orgins of their own arts for thousands of years. [9] (Which, for the record, does not mean that the martial arts are a worthless activity. It's simply that, like all human endeavors, a lot of nonsense has gotten absorbed into them throughout history. In fact, I've been studying martial arts, off and on, my entire adult life, and I think they're great! [10])

Still, the wise old teacher ploy is not for everyone. If you wish to run a New Age seminar and just can't bring yourself to invent a suitable guru, then there are other options. Channeling, of course, is considered a valid and completely nonverifiable source for information, but it is not the only one. You may try any of these other fine scams, all firmly grounded in metaphysical mumbo jumbo.

If you wish to promote reincarnation, then you may use "past life memories" as the source. Some New Agers prefer to make reference to such things as "ancestral memories," "trace memories," or "the old soul." Ancestral memories are memories of your ancestors that have been passed down to you. Strange how the psychologists still haven't been able to discover them. Trace memories, as they were explained to me, are similar to ancestral memories except they don't really have to come from your ancestors. You can sort of pick them up from animals and other outside sources, and they exist kind of floating on the fringes of all your other memories inside your head. The old soul is different because the memories don't come from your memory; instead they come to you via your soul direct from "the old soul," which is a big old "shared soul/higher consciousness" that everything living can tap into.

If this doesn't make any sense to you, don't worry. It isn't sup-

posed to. Besides, most New Agers don't really give too much
thought to these things anyway, and you can usually just get away
with spitting out the proper buzzwords that will make them comfortable and relaxed. If anyone questions you closely as to the truth
of these doctrines, then tell them knowingly that they are self-evident
to the enlightened and besides, this is how animals obtained
instincts. [11] If that fails, then say, "Please, let's respect one another's

opinions and views. There's no need to argue." That last cop-out virtually always works with New Agers as you steal their money.

Yet these ploys lack the charisma of that tried-and-true source of mystical teachings, the old master or the all-knowing teacher. Do yourself a favor and develop a teacher if you wish to pull these schemes off well.

ENDNOTES

1   For whatever reason, therapists of all types generally advertise extensively in these newsletters. It's my firm belief that most therapists are quacks and likely to be dangerous. I expect that this is doubly true of New Age-oriented therapists who often have a tendency to fly off on bizarre tangents as they utilize strange, trendy, unproven fad treatments.

    If you or someone you know are considering going to a therapist for help with a problem, you really should consult the book *Beware the Talking Cure* by Terrance Gardner. Written by a therapist, it's practically a consumer's guide to what to look for and beware of when hiring members of this profession.

2   As I sit here rereading this, I'm reminded of what I found in today's local paper. A "psychic" (shady credentials) who is also an "author" (very shady credentials!) is giving a talk at a local New Age "fellowship." Her credentials are that she's said to have had two near-death experiences. Admission is $8 per person. I wonder if she'd consider making her medical records available to the public? Furthermore, where else can you get ahead by being accident-prone?

3   The author wishes to have it on record that he has nothing against either Tibetans or American Indians. In fact, one of the reasons I find this saintly idealization of Indians and Tibetans to be quite irksome is due to my having participated in some heavy drinking sessions with members of both groups. By the end of these, none present seemed to be particularly enlightened, although I did learn some neat insults and curses used by both groups (i.e., never call your Tibetan guru a Bangladeshi fisherman or tell him his father is a carpenter; he won't like it).

4   For an overview of the entire genre of "magical autobiography," an excellent source is the essay, "Armchair Shamanism: A Yankee Way of Knowledge" in *The Fringes of Reason: A Whole Earth Catalog*. For information specifically on Castaneda's works, see *Castaneda's Journey* and *The Don Juan Papers* by Richard de Mille.

5   See *Ancient Wisdom Revived: A History of the Theosophical Movement* by Bruce Campbell, 1980, University of California Press. Unfortunately this is out of print, but the story is also told in L. Sprague DeCamp's very interesting work, *Lost Continents*.

6   Remember in the last chapter where we taught you how to produce an irregular heartbeat at the wrist by applying pressure on the brachial artery that supplies its blood flow? It's quite possible that Blavatsky knew this trick too. Upon reading Gertrude Marvin William's biography, *Madame Blavatsky: Priestess of the Occult* (Alfred A. Knopf, 1946), I was impressed with the way in which she would frequently avoid confrontations or disputes with her lackeys by suddenly falling ill and being confined to her bed, particularly later in life (which also happened to be when her followers were becoming more and more disillusioned with her organization). Often while stuck in bed, Blavatsky would exhibit an irregular heartbeat when someone checked her pulse. This would generally lead to an outpouring of sympathy or concern, and the followers would agree to stay.

7   Among these are the Theosophists, the Rosicrucians, the I AM movement, and the Acquarian Foundation of British Columbia, Canada. Some of these groups flourished in the 1920s and 1930s, but others still exist. Details are scarce and hard to come by. One source is the chapter "The Hidden Masters Revealed" in the book *Subterranean Worlds* by Walter Kafton-Minkel. The idea still exists, and curiously, played a key role in the plot of the second season of the quirky television show *Twin Peaks*.

8   For details on Hoskin and his exposure, see "The Third Eye" in *The Skeptical Inquirer*, Fall 1987, pp. 29–32, or "The 'Lama' from London" in *The Fringes of Reason*, p. 48.

9   For example, see Michael F. Spiesbach's article "Bodhidharma: Meditating Monk or Master of Make Believe?" in *The Journal of Asian Martial Arts,* Vol. 1, Number 4, 1992, and Robert W. Young's "The History and Development of Tae Kyon," Vol. 2, Number 2, 1993, of the same publication, which gives a good history of all major contemporary Korean martial arts while being careful to separate fact from legend.

10   This in itself is one of those really cool claims that's surprisingly easy to make and fits almost within the realm of this book. In order to "study the martial arts, off and on, for your entire adult life," begin to study at age 18, then stop when you get bored. When you start up again, suddenly you've been studying off and on your entire adult life!

11   Personal communication from Mark Shammon, scholar, gentleman, author, and iconoclast.

Hey You! Don't Read the Stars! Read This Book Instead!

Creating an Astrology Column

Suddenly the furious pilgrim rose to his feet and, with a mighty blow of his fist, he smote the flippant guru.

"Ouch!" cried the guru as he fell backward, spilling his beer into the snow. "Why'd you do that?"

"Because you're full of shit, that's why!" and then the pilgrim stormed off into the sunset.

"Wait! Where are you going?" cried the guru.

"To find another guru and another mountain," screamed the furious pilgrim as he stormed off into the snow . . .

Here's an introduction to astrology in a nutshell. Don't blink.

The things that everyone should know about astrology are:

1. Astrology doesn't work.

2. The motions of the moon and the planets don't affect human behavior.
3. Astrology makes a great many predictions about many things all at the same time.
4. People who believe in astrology tend to remember the successful predictions and forget the rest.
5. Some people like to use astrology to plan their lives. Although astrology doesn't really work, they feel comforted by having some sort of help in making their daily decisions. Although the advice received is vague and often contradictory, the belief that it is useful advice provides comfort, guidance, and a feeling of spiritual connection to the people who use it.
6. Such people are not necessarily bad, but they are incorrect when they say astrology is true.
7. Astrology is most certainly not a science.

"What?" cry the believers. "You can't say that! You must provide evidence."

Fair enough. Let's look at some astronomical facts.

Because the stars and the planets are very, very far away, their gravitational effects and, even more importantly, the changes in their gravitational affects, are very small, so there is no possible way that it could work.

Although it is widely believed that the phases of the moon influence human behavior, this belief is not proven by statistical analysis. For example, although many ambulance attendants and crisis hot line volunteers believe that they are busier on the nights when there is a full moon, the actual number of calls and emergencies does not seem to be affected by the condition or perceived condition of the moon. In fact, although I believed this myself for many years, it is simply not true. And if the nearby moon doesn't change our behavior, what can the far away planets do? Mercy goodness! It appears that *humanity alone* is responsible for the behavior of humanity! As this is a frightening thought, thus lies the appeal of the ancient psychological crutch known as astrology.

So much for the "science" behind astrology. Beyond the above facts, there really isn't much more that can be said to connect the two. In fact, virtually all astronomers disbelieve in astrology, and most become extremely annoyed when people confuse the two.

Nevertheless, it's the same old thing once again. People believe what they wish to believe because it makes them feel good, not necessarily because it's true. People tend to believe in astrology due to the fact that it makes a great deal of vague predictions about a great many things all at once. These predictions provide comfort to believers.

A good astrologer can make big bucks. Furthermore, due to the nature of the New Age movement, a practitioner of almost any other "art" will find that an occasional knowing reference to astrology will often add greatly to their image. As astrological believers tend to come under a great deal of criticism from people like myself, your professed belief in astrology can help put them at ease. Then, after they feel relaxed and comfortable, you can trick them into giving you their money.

Professional psychics use astrology all the time. Why? I don't know. I would think that a true psychic would be the last person who would have any use for astrology, even if it were true. Nevertheless, not too long ago an acquaintance of mine and I tried to test the powers of a self-proclaimed psychic who had volunteered for us. At one point in the test, she tried to wriggle out of the procedure by claiming (inaccurately we later discovered) that the astrological conditions were not right. [1] Time and time again, image is everything; reality is nothing in the world of paranormal scams.

Therefore, we'll offer the following tips for those who wish to obtain a reputation as being well-informed in astrological principles. If someone you know has a newsletter (for whatever cause) or newspaper, offer to write an astrology column. It's easier than an advice column and just as well received.

The simplest, although not necessarily the easiest, means to pass oneself off as an astrologer is to actually go out and learn astrology. Study long and hard from esoteric works of astrological teachings.

NO HOGWASH!

Our motto is RESULTS! And our record speaks for itself! Yes, it's Magick, but it works like science!

Everyone has a life situation they want to change. Our purpose is to help YOU change YOURS. People just like YOU are finding new handles on life and getting happily ahead by applying the Universal Principles brought in such easy to use form by   through E.S.P.

Our Super Self Help Programs feature the Magickal Ministry of   D.D., In combination with the Marvelous Mediumship of

The   20 published books are all available, including   (A latest, Self Help Manual for Mule Headed People)," and

Memorize large sections of complex tables that carefully describe the perceived positions of the visible planets and stars. True astrology is, if nothing else, quite complicated, and this is one of the reasons it has been so popular over the centuries. With all the statements it provides, something, somewhere that has been predicted is bound to occur.

Of course, it's important to remember that few astrology columnists actually use all of this data. After all, they should be the first to admit that they are only generalizing when they create the columns. Therefore, it seems that if you aren't going to use this information, why go to the effort of learning how to acquire it?

An easier way to do it is to take about a weeks worth of astrology columns from a newspaper. Cut them apart so that you have 12 for each day. This should leave you with 84 different statements. Put them in a jar. Simply pull them out, one at a time, and paste at random. Be careful not to run the same column in the same place too often, but generally speaking, it's safe to place what was once a Leo piece over in the Sagittarius spot or make similar moves.

Don't hesitate to reword statements and change things around a bit. Change positive statements to negative statements. In fact, this is probably a good idea anyway, as it avoids copyright problems. (Although I suppose if you were dragged into court, you could simply argue that you looked at the same stars they did and achieved the same results. I'm sure you'll lose, but it sounds logical. Let me know if you try this.)

This should be enough to get you started until you get the hang of writing your own. But don't get carried away. Never say, "You will find a $20 bill on the sidewalk." That is too specific and easy to disprove. Besides, it's hardly mystical sounding, and in the world of the paranormal, image is everything. (Remember, if you think that you really can predict the future, then you should either see a doctor to get your head checked or else stop messing around with astrology buffs and invest in the stock market.) Instead, say something like, "You will encounter the opportunity for fortune today if you keep your outlook broad."

The advantages of this approach are many. First of all, it's vague. Secondly, it's suitably weird and mystical. Thirdly, it's difficult to impossible to prove whether it happened or not. If somebody comes to you and says, "Hey, I got mugged on the day you said I would encounter the opportunity for fortune," simply suggest that they are now eminently qualified to write a book about their mishap, sell the movie rights, or appear on a talk show. Or perhaps they could teach crime prevention seminars or organize a victims' recovery movement. If they don't fall for this, then simply turn the blame on them. Explain that they did not receive their opportunity for fortune because their "outlook" was not sufficiently "broad" at the time the opportunity should have been encountered.

Use your imagination. Tell people what they want to hear. Tell them they are underappreciated. Tell them their lives will improve. Give them hope. They will love you for it. Then you can crush them and steal their money.

Nevertheless, don't get carried away. An astrology column should not be an end in itself. In fact, it's kind of a nowhere activity unless you use it to move on to bigger and better things. Use it as a tool to impress potential high-paying private clients. Advertise your 1-900 number in your astrology column. Whenever possible, work your way onto television.

Many people insist that it's their right to believe in astrology even though it can be proven false. Respect their rights. Then rip them off and steal their money. Sure it's immoral and rotten, but just remember, you won't be the first.

ENDNOTES

1   This person also claimed the ability to see auras, talk to ghosts, and do past-life regressions as well as the ability to utilize astrology and ESP to aid her clients. Her powers, in short, seemed to parallel whatever the public might wish them to be at any given moment. Don't laugh! She drives a much nicer car than I do.

But Seriously Folks . . .

The guru picked himself up off of the snow and brushed the pile of spilled chicken wings off of his lap. He watched, befuddled, as the pilgrim continued his march off into the sunset.

As the pilgrim crossed over the horizon, never to be seen again, the guru grunted to himself, "Well, whatta ya know? You can expose some people to the truth, but they just won't accept it."

And then he said these words of wisdom: "Before you can understand the universe, you must first understand yourself."

With that, he sat back down, turned toward television, pulled out another beer, and reached for some more wings.

If you've read this far, then you've learned a lot of interesting affects and dirty tricks. Knowledge is power, and you can now go out and commit a great deal of mayhem if you're so inclined. If you practice, you can fool a lot of people into believing that you, and the entire world for that matter, are something that they are not, possessed of seemingly superhuman powers and miraculous happenings. With a little luck, a great deal of dishonesty, and a dose of socially manipulative behavior, there's little limit to the problems you could create.

For this very reason, someone sooner or later is going to ask the very valid question of whether this was a worthwhile book to write and if perhaps it would have been better to keep the information hidden.

I answer such critics thusly. In writing this book, I have created very little that is original. The information presented is already out there. I've merely made it a little more accessible and presented it in hopefully a more palatable and easier-to-understand manner. If people misuse it, then this is their decision and it is on their conscience. I, most certainly, do not approve. If nothing else, through the frequent references to theft and mayhem, I hope that I have helped drive home the point, often ignored by the media, that paranormal hoaxes and supernatural claims are often much more than simple "entertainment."

I sincerely believe that if people become aware that such frauds are not only possible but occur regularly and use this information to increase their awareness, then I will have done some good in the world. It is my hope that I have succeeded in bringing readers to a newer and more sophisticated understanding of how at least some of the paranormal gurus out there work and make their money. Since people are actively misusing this information already, then I feel this book is a valid and much needed product. By showing how easy it is to falsely create convincing "evidence" of such phenomena, you can be on the lookout for it.

Keep in mind, however, that simply because something cannot be explained by the techniques in this book doesn't mean it's not hoaxed. Hoaxing, and its sister science of counterfeiting, are forever engaged in a running technological race with legitimate society. When a hoaxer finds that one method of doing things is uncovered and made public, then he and his colleagues will inevitably create another one.

Throughout this work, I've focused on the small-scale harmful effects of paranormal fraud. People steal each other's money and con one another into believing nonsense. Years of people's lives are wasted studying foolishness that was invented by a charlatan trying to make a fast buck. Individuals are recruited into believing unhealthy and harmful ideologies and often absorbed into strange cults. Sometimes, families are broken up for this very reason.

It's difficult to pass laws against such things, particularly in a free society. Even when such legislation is in place, it inevitably has so many loopholes and such low priority among law enforcement that its usefulness is limited. Many would argue that on the basis of libertarian ideologies, it would not even be desirable to censor or restrict paranormal, supernatural, and pseudoscientific claims. To do so would be to violate our cherished rights to free speech and even freedom of religion. Many would further argue that people should be free to choose and purchase products as they see fit, and believe and live as they so choose, even if they are being unhealthily deceived and manipulated by someone else. Such people argue that society should allow free reign to business and entrepreneurship, and those who suffer because of it deserve their fate. Even if this cold attitude is valid, then few would disagree that we have a humanitarian duty to at least try to educate and warn those who are likely to fall prey to the unwholesome manipulations of others. If we don't make this effort, then we are not so much a free society as merely an unhealthy collection of depraved cynics and sociopaths. In order to help others, we must, first, educate ourselves.

When we look at the big picture, paranormal fraud can cause serious problems for society. When police on a high-profile case are pressured into following the "leads" of a phony psychic, time, money, and energy are diverted from more fruitful leads. When a hoaxer convinces scientists to look seriously into his or her "abilities," he wastes the time of some very talented people. Not only that, but generally such research is not done for free. Somebody has to pay for it, be it a university, the government, a corporation, or a grant from a nonprofit educational or charitable foundation. Thousands of dollars, if not more, is easily diverted from other, more useful pursuits, including technological research, medicinal cures, and so on.

This financial cost ultimately is passed on to the public somehow. The delay in discovering beneficial products and technologies further harms the public.

I've used as much humor (tasteful or otherwise) as possible in this book. Yet when the president of the United States has his schedule secretly adjusted behind the scenes by his wife on orders from an astrologer, and not even the Secret Service knows the real reason, things just aren't funny anymore.

We live in a world with many problems: encroaching global overpopulation and the social problems, riots, genocidal conflicts, and civil wars that come from overcrowding; new and frightening diseases; the constant threat of environmental imbalances and widespread global extinctions; the horrifying technological side effects of deadly toxins and pollutants; and widespread proliferation of nuclear, biological, and chemical weapons of mass destruction. It is no exaggeration to say that for the first time in our collective history, humankind has entered a period in which it could easily destroy itself, accidentally or on purpose, through one means or another.

I believe that we, the human race, can make it through these times and collectively move on to whatever bigger and better destiny awaits us. To do this, however, the most important resource that we will need is our brains and our rationality. We need to analyze our world, our universe, and our problems and then work to fix them accordingly. The presence of a variety of irrational movements that believe that our problems can be solved through mystical mumbo-jumbo, divine intervention, and unthinking emotionality does nothing to help understand or fix the problems that we face. As such movements are fueled, at least in part, by hoaxing—assisted by the amazing human desire to rationalize whatever it chooses to believe—a good first step toward increasing rationality is to begin exposing such hoaxers and holding them up to scrutiny.

Did I just make the claim that the fate of the world depends on our ability to detect and expose paranormal fraud? Strangely enough, I believe I just did. Or, more accurately, what I said was that our ability to understand the world around us and then work effectively to fix its problems depends ultimately on our ability to distinguish fact from fiction and reality from fantasy. And this is why we all should be alert to the possibility of a hoax when we read about a claim of the miraculous and the fabulous.

And besides, lest I suffer from getting too heavy after ten chapters of trying to keep things light, learning about hoaxes is fun. With all the problems in the world, I believe we should all do our part to make the world a better place. On the other hand, I also believe that you might as well try to work on a cause that you find satisfying or just plain enjoyable. After all, although it's good to do something, you can't do everything, so find a cause that you enjoy. If nothing else, it will keep you motivated.

Detractors are going to cry that this work is cynical and one-sided. To these people I say, "Yeah, so what? It's just one book. If you don't like it, then buy a dozen copies and burn them!" I've never claimed to be 100 percent correct on everything I say. (Well, okay, I have, but I couldn't get anybody else to agree with me.) You don't have to agree with me, my approach, or everything I say to get some benefit from this work. My only hope is that the next time you see or hear of something extraordinary and unearthly, you'll view it in a slightly different way. The next time you run across a flyer offering a seminar on past-life therapies or a bestseller about the latest outbreak of UFO sightings or an advertisement for the latest psychic hot line or other supernatural panacea, the best approach is to look at it with an open mind, yet use some of the ideas presented in this book as part of your intellectual and analytical tools. You can, after all, be both open minded and ask for proof.

Appendix

1

Firewalking

For a variety of reasons, it was decided to leave firewalking out of the main body of text. Nevertheless, this book would be lacking without some sort of description of this peculiar and misunderstood phenomenon.

First of all, firewalking is not so much walking on fire as it is walking on hot coals. The hot coals are spread along the ground and the participants, normally barefoot, trod across them slowly but steadily. When the walk is over, surprisingly they are unharmed and their feet unburned.

Although many claim that the process indicates a human power to defy reality through a process of mind over matter, physicists feel otherwise.

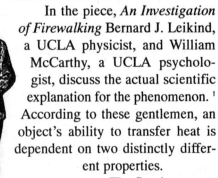

In the piece, *An Investigation of Firewalking* Bernard J. Leikind, a UCLA physicist, and William McCarthy, a UCLA psychologist, discuss the actual scientific explanation for the phenomenon. [1] According to these gentlemen, an object's ability to transfer heat is dependent on two distinctly different properties.

The first is temperature, or how hot the object is. The second is thermal conductivity. This distinction is significant because, although objects made of different materials may be of the same temperature, they have different abilities to take this "hotness" and transfer it to a second object. For example, if you put a metal pan full of food in an oven and bake it at 500 degrees, soon the air, the pan, and the food will all be 500 degrees in temperature. If you put a bare hand into the oven air quickly, however, chances are it will not get burned. Yet if you touch the 500-degree pan, it will hurt. The reason is that metal transfers heat more quickly and easily than air.

The same thing is true of wood. One can walk quickly across hot coals without getting burned. Yet if you were to walk slowly across the coals or lie upon them for any significant length of time, you would be burned no matter how hard you concentrated.

Of course, it's much more exciting to believe that mind over matter is responsible for the phenomenon, so it's no surprise that the physics explanation has been disputed by many. In an effort to reinforce the physics solution, Bernard Leikind once went on a firewalk with pieces of raw meat strapped to the bottoms of his feet. The fact that the unthinking and consciousness-lacking steaks did not burn reinforces his view. [2]

Despite this, the idea that firewalking somehow defies the laws of nature holds a great appeal to many. To reinforce the glamour and excitement of the process, such walks are normally held at night, where the coals appear brighter and more intense in the darkness. The atmosphere is often festive and otherworldly, with organizers initiating chants, giving motivational speeches, and hawking their latest self-improvement courses.

Is it harmless? A friend of mine doesn't think so. Impressed by a firewalk, he promptly signed up for one of the subsequent self-improvement courses and wound up wasting several hundred dollars and a great deal of time. Additionally, Leikind and McCarthy recount the tale of how on one firewalk they visited, a physically challenged woman, unable to walk at normal speed, decided to make the walk using a cane. She and the organizers both believed that her willpower could protect her from the coals. Instead, physics being physics and thus inflexible, she burned her bare feet badly due to her lengthy contact with the coals.

The moral of the story: don't play with fire unless you understand what you're doing!

ENDNOTES

1   This piece originally appeared in *Skeptical Inquirer*, Vol. 10, No. 1, Fall 1985. It has been reprinted and included as part of the book *The Hundredth Monkey*, edited by Kendrick Frazier (Prometheus Books, Amherst, NY).

2   Bernard Leikind, "Is Raw Meat Conscious?" in *Skeptic*, Vol. 3, No. 1, page 108. This firewalk was filmed and aired on an episode of "Mysterious Forces Beyond" on cable's "The Learning Channel."

Appendix

Some Periodicals and Organizations of Note

The following are some periodicals that cover many of the issues discussed in this book. Prices and all other information are, of course, subject to change without notice.

The Skeptical Inquirer
Box 703
Amherst, NY 14226-0703

This bimonthly magazine is often available at large newsstands. It is the official publication of the Committee for the Scientific Investigation of Claims of the Paranormal (CSICOP), an organization of scientists and scientifically inclined people who are interested and generally concerned about paranormal, supernatural, and pseudoscientific claims. The magazine generally consists half of articles that critique and explain various claims and half of lofty, philosophical pieces discussing (in negative terms) why people tend to believe in such claims. The organization maintains several facilities in the Buffalo, New York, area, including a library, services to

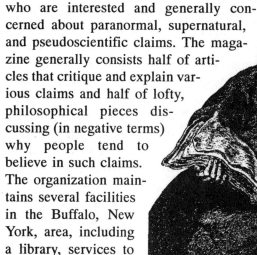

the media, and files of clippings. It also publishes a second quarterly newsletter that deals mostly with news in and around CSICOP itself. It offers all back issues of the magazine for sale and keeps such issues in print. Although *Skeptical Inquirer* tends to be stuffy and intellectual, with most of the contributors having Ph.D.s (and showing it!), it is an invaluable source of information that is often unavailable anywhere else. In short, although it can be a lot of work to read, being exposed to a few issues can be an eye-opening experience.

Besides, lest I've been too negative, they do publish pieces by yours truly on a fairly regular basis. I have no regrets about having discovered this magazine, and I eagerly read each issue.

A one-year, six-issue subscription is available for $29.50. One free sample copy is available upon request.

Skeptic
2761 N. Marengo Ave.
Altadena, CA 91001

This quarterly magazine is the official publication of the Skeptics Society, a newer, younger organization with goals similar to CSICOP, and is occasionally found at larger newsstands. Although the magazine was originally quite similar to *Skeptical Inquirer* in content, it seems to have been breaking off in its own unique direction with an increased interest in strange claims in the social sciences and on the margins of society. For example, recent issues have dealt with Holocaust denial, AIDS conspiracy theories, the politics of alternative medicine, and issues concerning I.Q. and race. Once again, the magazine tends to be very heavy reading, but it is an invaluable source of otherwise hard-to-get information. Back issues are available, as are audio and videotapes of various lectures the group has held at its meetings. It is a fine piece of work.

A one-year, four-issue subscription is available for $35, $25 for students and seniors, and includes membership in the Skeptics Society.

Some Periodicals and Organizations of Note

The Fortean Times
Box 2409
London NW5 4NP UK

U.S. subscriptions:
P.O. Box 754
Manhasset, NY 11030-0754

Fortean Times is significantly different from the magazines mentioned above in form, style, and intent. Named after Charles Fort, an eccentric writer who devoted his life to collecting newspaper clippings of strange phenomenon and then using them to belittle the scientific establishment, *Fortean Times* bills itself as "The Magazine of Strange Phenomena." Each bimonthly issue contains a wide variety of articles devoted to reporting, explaining, discussing, and popularizing strange ideas and happenings. Although I often disagree with the contents of specific articles, each issue contains enough bizarre, amusing, and informative stuff that I always get a kick out of it. Furthermore, it includes enough in-depth articles exposing hoaxes and false reports to keep me satisfied that the staff does, in fact, value knowing the truth about such things. Although not quite as concerned with accuracy as *Skeptical Inquirer* or *Skeptic, Fortean Times* is often a lot more fun to read. Occasionally found on large newsstands.

A one-year, six-issue subscription is available for $30 or 12 pounds in the United Kingdom.

Fate
P.O. Box 1940
170 Future Way
Marion, OH 43305-1940

Fate, published monthly and available on most newsstands, is the granddaddy of all paranormal magazines. It always contains an amazing assortment of articles that makes one wonder just how far people will go before they come to their senses. If you think I have exaggerated when I state that some people will believe almost anything, then you haven't read *Fate* magazine. Worth reading, at least once or twice, just to get a complete picture of the paranormal scene. Also, the ads provide a good source for checking on trends and such.

The above are merely some of the many magazines that cover these topics. Many others come and go. A trip to a good newsstand (the larger, the better) will reveal more of interest. Furthermore, there are many organizations devoted to paranormal subjects, and these come with an incredible variety of ideologies, levels of sophistication, and goals. Most have some newsletter or publication or a computer web site of some sort. Many of these organizations, their mailing addresses, and a brief description are listed in publications such as *The Directory of Associations*, a standard reference work available at most good libraries. Contact the organizations themselves for details about their purpose and intent (and interesting stuff in your mailbox).

I would be completely remiss if I did not include mention of such fine magazines as *Scientific American* and *Discover*. One of the benefits of taking a skeptical approach to the paranormal is that once you begin to learn why these claims are not accepted by science, you also begin to learn what science is and just how wondrous and fascinating the universe around us can be. I've never regretted it.

The following organizations are serious groups that, although not devoted to paranormal claims per se, deal with important issues that often figure prominently in paranormal claims. I support them all.

False Memory Syndrome Foundation
3401 Market Street, Suite 130
Philadelphia, PA 19104

This organization is devoted to the very serious problem of persons who, through bad psychotherapy or other means, come to false conclusions about their past. These occur when said persons are led to "recover" forgotten memories either under hypnosis or other circumstances. These memories often prove to be inaccurate.

Such false memories often occur in cases of alleged UFO abductions, past lives and reincarnation research, and, most tragically, allegations of early childhood sexual molestation. The latter cases are particularly upsetting because not only are they the most easily believed, they also involve accusing innocent people of unspeakable crimes.

Although the False Memory Syndrome Foundation has come under a great deal of fire from its opponents, it has a great many psychologists, psychiatrists, and psychotherapists on its board of directors, and it does a lot of good work for those families who have been struck by the false accusations that surround false memories. It also works to educate professionals, academics, and others as to how memory works and how false memories can be caused and prevented.

Info-Cult
Resource Center on Cultic Thinking
5655 Park Avenue, Suite 208
Montreal, Quebec
Canada H2V 4H2

Although the more famous Cult Awareness Network has recently gone bankrupt following a series of harassing lawsuits, I have been told that many of the services it once offered will now be provided by the above organization. Information and referral services regarding cults and cult-like organizations are available from Info-Cult in both French and English.

Cult Awareness Network of New York and New Jersey
(Citizen's Freedom Foundation)
P.O. Box 867
Teaneck, NJ 07666

The Cult Awareness Network of New York and New Jersey, formerly a branch of the Cult Awareness Network, has informed me that they intend to take up much of the duties of the now defunct national organization. They will offer services to people regardless of their geographic location.

The James Randi Educational Foundation
201 S.E. Davie Blvd.
Ft. Lauderdale, FL 33316-1815

As I write, James Randi, the famous magician, author, investigator, and skeptic, has just formed his own educational foundation. It remains to be seen what the exact services offered by this organization will be, but the impression I am left with is that a great deal will involve offering information services over the internet. Mr. Randi also assures me that the foundation will offer funding assistance for research projects and legal aid for skeptics besieged by harassing lawsuits. The internet address is http://www.randi.org.

Bibliography

In an effort to increase the usefulness of this bibliography, an attempt has been made to divide books by category. Many of these works could easily be placed in several categories. Works that were particularly useful or likely to be enjoyed by readers of this book are noted with an asterisk.

Books Primarily on or Critical of Psychic Phenomena

Anderson, John, with Rich Monk. *Psychic Phenomena Revealed.* Lafayette, LA: Huntington House. No Date.

Booth, John. *Psychic Paradoxes.* Buffalo, NY: Prometheus Books. 1984.

* Fuller, Uriah (Karl Fulves). *Confessions of a Psychic: The Secret Notebooks of Uriah Fuller.* Teaneck, NJ: Karl Fulves. No Date.

* Fuller, Uriah (Karl Fulves). *Further Confessions of a Psychic: The Secret Notebooks of Uriah Fuller.* Teaneck, NJ: Karl Fulves. 1980.

Gardner, Martin. *How Not to Test a Psychic.* Buffalo, NY: Prometheus Books. 1989.

* Marks, David, and Richard Kammann. *The Psychology of the Psychic.* Buffalo, NY: Prometheus Books. 1980.

* Randi, James. *The Truth About Uri Geller.* Buffalo, NY: Prometheus Books. 1975, 1982.

Books on or Critical of UFO Phenomena

Festinger, Leon, Henry M. Riecken, and Stanley Schachter. *When Prophecy Fails: A Social and Psychological Study of a Modern Group that Predicted the Destruction of the World.* New York: Harper & Row. 1956.

* Klass, Phillip J. *UFO Abductions: A Dangerous Game.* Buffalo, NY: Prometheus Books. 1989.

* Peebles, Curtis. *Watch the Skies! A Chronicle of the Flying Saucer Myth.* Washington and London: Smithsonian Institution Press. 1994.

* Sheaffer, Robert. *The UFO Verdict: Examining the Evidence.* Buffalo, NY: Prometheus Books. 1986.

* Spencer, John and Hillary Evans (editors). *Phenomenon: Forty Years of Flying Saucers.* New York: Avon Books. 1988.

Books on or Critical of the New Age, Fortune-Telling, or Astrology

Baer, Randall N. *Inside the New Age Nightmare.* Lafayette, LA: Huntington House. 1989.

* Basil, Robert (editor). *Not Necessarily the New Age.* Buffalo, NY: Prometheus Books. 1988.

Fergunson, Marilyn. *The Aquarian Conspiracy: Personal and Social Transformation in Our Time.* New York: Jeremy P.

Tarcher/Perigee Books. 1980, 1987.

* Gordon, Henry. *Channeling into the New Age: The "Teachings" of Shirley MacLaine and Other Such Gurus.* Buffalo, NY: Prometheus Books. 1988.

* Rae, Alexander C. *Bluff Your Way at Fortune Telling.* Sussex, England: Ravette Books. 1988.

Books on or Critical of General Paranormal Phenomena

* DeCamp, L. Sprague. *Lost Continents.* New York, NY: Dover Books. 1954, 1970.

* DeMille, Richard. *The Don Juan Papers: Further Castaneda Controversies.* Santa Barbara, CA: Ross Erikson. 1980.

* Gardner, Martin. *Fads and Fallacies in the Name of Science.* New York: Dover. 1952, 1957.

Gardner, Martin. *Science: Good, Bad, and Bogus.* New York: Avon. 1981.

Harris, Melvin. *Investigating the Unexplained.* Buffalo, NY: Prometheus Books. 1986.

* Kafton-Mindel, Walter. *Subterranean Worlds: 100,000 Years of Dragons, Dwarfs, the Dead, Lost Races, and UFOs from Inside the Earth.* Port Townsend, WA: Loompanics Unlimited. 1989.

* Keene, Lamar M., as told to Allen Spraggert. *The Psychic Mafia.* New York: Dell. 1976.

* Leung Ting. *Skills of the Vagabonds*. Hong Kong: Leung's Publications. 1983. (Note: Often available from martial arts supply dealers.)

* Leung Ting. *Skills of the Vagabonds II: Behind the Incredibles*. Hong Kong: Leung's Publications. 1991.

* Nickell, Joe, with John F. Fischer. *Secrets of the Supernatural: Investigating the World's Occult Mysteries*. Buffalo, NY: Prometheus Books. 1988.

* Nickell, Joe. *Looking for a Miracle: Weeping Icons, Relics, Stigmata, Visions, and Healing Cures*. Buffalo, NY: Prometheus Books. 1993.

* Nickell, Joe. *Entities: Angels, Spirits, Demons, and Other Alien Beings*. Buffalo, NY: Prometheus Books. 1995. (Note: Joe Nickell has written many other fine books on investigating various paranormal claims.)

* Randi, James. *Flim-Flam! Psychics, ESP, Unicorns, and Other Delusions*. Buffalo, NY: Prometheus Books. 1982.

* Randi, James. *The Faith Healers*. Buffalo, NY: Prometheus Books. 1989.

* Schultz, Ted (editor). *The Fringes of Reason: A Whole Earth Catalog*. New York: Harmony Books. 1989.

Scott, Reginald. *The Discoverie of Witchcraft*. New York: Dover Books. No Date (reprint of a work from 1584).

Books on or about Magic, Sleight of Hand, or Conjuring

Earle, Lee. *The Classic Reading: An Introduction to the Gentle Art of Cold Reading*. Binary Star Publications. 1989, 1990, 1992 (book and audio tape).

Hopkins, Albert A. *Magic: Stage Illusions, Special Effects, and Trick Photography*. New York: Dover. 1898, 1976.

Houdin, Robert. *King of the Conjurers: Memoirs of Robert Houdin*. New York: Dover. 1964.

* Jillette, Penn and Teller. *Cruel Tricks for Dear Friends*. New York: Villard Books. 1991.

* Jillette, Penn and Teller. *How to Play with Your Food*. New York: Villard Books. 1992.

Nelms, Henning. *Magic and Showmanship: A Handbook for Conjurers*. New York: Dover. 1969.

Saville, Thomas K., and Herb Dewey. *Red Hot Cold Reading: The Professional Pseudo Psychic*. (No date or publisher. Available through magic specialty suppliers.)

Books on or about Hoaxes, Scams, and Swindles

Gibson, Walter B. (editor). *The Fine Art of Swindling*. New York: Grosset and Dunlop. 1966.

* Henderson, M. Allen. *Flim-Flam Man: How Con Games Work*. Boulder, CO: Paladin Press. 1985.

* Henderson, M. Allen. *Money for Nothing: Rip Offs, Cons, and Swindles*. Boulder, CO: Paladin Press. 1986.

MacDougall, Curtis D. *Hoaxes.* New York: Dover Books. 1940, 1958, 1968.

Marlock, Dennis, and John Dowling. *License to Steal: Traveling Con Artists—Their Games, Their Rules, Your Money.* Boulder, CO: Paladin Press. 1994.

Mott, Graham M. *Scams, Swindles, and Rip-Offs: Personal Stories and Powerful Lessons.* Littleton, CO: Golden Shadows Press. 1993, 1994.

* Randi, James. *An Encyclopedia of Claims, Frauds, and Hoaxes of the Occult and Supernatural.* New York: St. Martin's Press. 1995.

* Reuther, Catherine (editor). *RE/Search #11: Pranks!* San Francisco: RE/Search Publications. 1987. (Dementedly funny!)

Santoro, Victor. *The Rip-Off Book.* Port Townsend, WA: Loompanics Unlimited. 1984.

Santoro, Victor. *Frauds, Rip-Offs, and Con Games.* Port Townsend, WA: Loompanics Unlimited. 1988.

Santoro, Victor. *Economic Sodomy: How Modern Frauds Work and How to Protect Yourself.* Port Townsend, WA: Loompanics Unlimited. 1994.

* Stein, Gordon and Marie J. MacNee. *Hoaxes! Dupes, Dodges, and Other Dastardly Deceptions.* Washington, DC: Visible Ink. 1995.

Books on or about the Psychology of Paranormal Phenomena or Belief

* Baker, Robert A. *They Call It Hypnosis.* Buffalo, NY: Prometheus Books. 1990.

* Baker, Robert A. *Hidden Memories: Voices and Visions from Within.* Buffalo, NY: Prometheus Books. 1992.

Benson, Herbert, and Miriam Z. Klipper. *The Relaxation Response.* New York: Avon. 1975.

Benson, Herbert, and William Proctor. *Beyond the Relaxation Response.* New York: Berkley Books. 1984.

* Galanter, Marc. *Cults: Faith, Healing, and Coercion.* New York, London: Oxford University Press. 1989.

* Neher, Andrew. *The Psychology of Transcendence.* New York: Dover. 1980, 1990.

Rawcliffe, D.H. *Illusions and Delusions of the Supernatural and the Occult.* New York: Dover Books. 1959.

Reed, Graham. *The Psychology of Anomolous Experience.* New York: Dover Books. 1988.

Miscellaneous Books Used in the Preparation of this Work

Andrews, Lynne. *Medicine Woman.* New York: Harper & Row. 1981.

* Baker, Robert A., and Joe Nickell. *Missing Pieces: How to Investigate Ghosts, UFOs, Psychics, and Other Mysteries.* Buffalo, NY: Prometheus Books. 1992.

* Brunvand, Jan Harold. *The Vanishing Hitchhiker: Urban Legends and their Meanings*. London: Picador. 1983.

* Brunvand, Jan Harold. *The Choking Doberman and Other "New" Urban Legends*. New York: W.W. Norton & Company. 1984.

* Brunvand, Jan Harold. *Curses! Broiled Again! The Hottest Urban Legends Going*. New York: W.W. Norton & Company. 1989.

Eliade, Mircea. *Shamanism: Archaic Techniques of Ecstasy*. Princeton, NJ: Princeton University Press. 1964.

Gilbey, John F. *Secret Fighting Arts of the World*. Rutland, VT: Tuttle. 1963.

Gilbey, John F. *The Way of a Warrior*. Berkeley, CA: North Atlantic Books. 1982, 1992.

Greywhiskers, Fifi (translated from the Siamese Cat language by T. Lobsang Rampa). *Living with the Lama*. London: Corgi Books. 1964.

* Nickell, Joe. *Camera Clues: A Handbook for Photographic Investigation*. Lexington, KY: The University of Kentucky Press. 1994.

* Paulos, John Allen. *Innumeracy: Mathematical Illiteracy and Its Consequences*. New York: Vintage Books. 1988.

Rampa, T. Lobsang. *The Third Eye*. New York: Ballantine. 1956, 1958.

Rampa, T. Lobsang. *My Visit to Venus*. New Brunswick, NJ: Inner Light Publications. 1988.

Videos and Films

1992. *Expert Body Language: The Science of People Reading.* Intelligence Inc., San Mateo, CA. (Available from Paladin Press.)

1993. *Leap of Faith.* Paramount, Hollywood, CA.

* 1982. NOVA: *UFOs: Are We Alone?* WGBH, Boston, MA.

* 1994. NOVA: *James Randi: The Secrets of the Psychics.* WGBH, Boston, MA.

* 1989. *Penn and Teller Get Killed.* Lorimar Film Company, Burbank, CA.

Periodicals

Ayers Sweat, Jane and Mark W. Durm. "Psychics: Do Police Departments Really Use Them?" *Skeptical Inquirer,* Vol. 17, No. 2, pp. 148–158.

Baker, Robert A. "The Aliens Among Us: Hypnotic Regression Revisited." *Skeptical Inquirer,* Vol. 12, No. 2, pp. 147–162.

Beyerstein, Barry. "The Myth of Alpha Consciousness." *Skeptical Inquirer,* Vol. 10, No. 1, pp. 23–35.

Beyerstein, Barry. "The Brain and Consciousness: Implications for Psi Phenomena." *Skeptical Inquirer,* Vol. 12, No. 2, pp. 163–173.

Clements, Warner. "Levitation: Some Phantasy and Some Physics." *Skeptical Inquirer,* Vol. 13, No. 3, pp. 289–295.

* Dean, Geoffrey. "Does Astrology Need to be True? Part 1: A Look at the Real Thing." *Skeptical Inquirer,* Vol. 11, No. 2, pp. 166–184.

* Dean, Geoffrey. "Does Astrology Need to be True? Part 2: The Answer is No." *Skeptical Inquirer,* Vol. 11, No. 3, pp. 257–273.

Dennett, Michael R. "Firewalking: Reality or Illusion." *Skeptical Inquirer,* Vol. 10, No. 1, pp. 36–40.

French, Christopher, Mandy Fowler, Katy McCarthy, and Debbie Peers. "Belief in Astrology: A Test of the Barnum Effect." *Skeptical Inquirer,* Vol. 15, No. 2, pp. 166–172.

* Gill, Samuel T. "Carrying the War into the Never-Never Land of Psi: Part 1." *Skeptical Inquirer,* Vol. 15, No. 3, pp. 269–273.

* Gill, Samuel T. "Carrying the War into the Never-Never Land of Psi: Part 2." *Skeptical Inquirer,* Vol. 15, No. 4, pp. 376–381. (Note: If you enjoyed this book, then you will probably enjoy Gill's very funny two-part article on how to pester and embarrass advocates of the paranormal.)

Hines, Terence M., and Todd Dennison. "A Reaction-Time Test of ESP and Precognition." *Skeptical Inquirer,* Vol. 13, No. 2, pp. 161–165.

Huston, Peter. "Night Terrors, Sleep Paralysis, and Devil-Stricken Telephone Cords from Hell." *Skeptic,* Vol. 17, No. 1, pp. 64–69.

Huston, Peter. "Elvis Impersonators: Is it Genetics, Environment, or in the Stars?" *Skeptical Inquirer,* Vol. 2, No. 3, pp. 50–52.

Klass, Phillip J. "Special Report: The MJ-12 Crashed Saucer Documents." *Skeptical Inquirer,* Vol. 12, No. 2, pp. 137–146.

* Leikind, Bernard J., and William J. McCarthy. "An Investigation of Firewalking." *Skeptical Inquirer*, Vol. 10, No. 1, pp. 23–34.

Lett, James. "A Field Guide to Critical Thinking." *Skeptical Inquirer*, Vol. 14, No. 2, pp. 153–160.

Nickell, Joe, and John F. Fischer. "The Crop Circle Phenomenon: An Investigative Report." *Skeptical Inquirer*, Vol. 16, No. 2, pp. 136–149.

Premanand, B. "Claims of Levitation 'Miracles' in India." *Skeptical Inquirer*, Vol. 13, No. 3, pp. 284–288.

Reed, Graham, "The Psychology of Channeling." *Skeptical Inquirer*, Vol. 13, No. 4, pp. 391–396.

Rowe, Walter F. "Psychic Detectives: A Critical Examination." *Skeptical Inquirer*, Vol. 17, No. 3, pp. 159–165.

Schultz, Ted. "The New Age: The Need for Myth in the Age of Science." *Skeptical Inquirer*, Vol. 13, No. 4, pp. 375–379.

Stein, Gordon. "The Lore of Levitation." *Skeptical Inquirer*, Vol. 13, No. 3, pp. 277–288.

Thomason, Sarah Grey. "'Entities' in the Linguistic Minefield." *Skeptical Inquirer*, Vol. 13, No. 4, pp. 391–396.

Wu Xiaoping. "Report of a Chinese Psychic's Pill Bottle Demonstration." *Skeptical Inquirer*, Vol. 13, No. 2, pp. 168–171.

Let the Blame Fall Where It May . . .

About the Author

Peter Huston's life has been a bizarre series of peculiar zigs and zags and unexpected twists and turns. He has been, at various times, an ambulance attendant, rock concert security guard, mental health residence counselor, teacher and tutor of English as a second language in Taiwan, and bobsled racer, among other things, and is currently striving to eke out a living as a free-lance writer when, in fact, the truth is that he's nothing more than an overeducated security guard/night watchman. Having spent more than three years living in Taiwan and bouncing around Asia, as well as having somehow earned a degree in Asian studies, he occasionally passes himself off as an Asian studies scholar. In this guise he wrote his first work, *Tongs, Gangs, and Triads: Chinese Crime Groups in North America*, published by Paladin Press. Occasionally, he exhibits a fondness for macho bullshit and has been known to do stupid things for the sake of seeing if they can be done.

Some years ago he became interested and concerned with the way in which paranormal phenomena is readily accepted by much of society, despite the flimsiness of most of the evidence. He has explored a variety of paranormal and supernatural claims, including Taiwanese spirit mediums, the Lake Champlain monster, sleep hallucinations, false memory syndrome, conspiracy theories, and Satanic cult hysteria. He has written on many of these subjects in magazines such as *Skeptical Inquirer* and *Skeptic*. He is vice president of the Inquiring Skeptics of Upper New York, an organization dedicated to exploring and publicizing information concerning paranormal claims from a skeptical point of view. At one time, he wrote a regular nonfiction column on such subjects for *Expanse,* a short-lived science fiction magazine with national distribution.

Huston was once, purely by accident, initiated into a secretive, underground Chinese religious group that is outlawed in the People's Republic of China and, until recently, Taiwan. They taught him magical techniques guaranteed to enable him to survive a fall from a flying airplane without a parachute. He has never tested these secret techniques, but he does remember them just in case. He can curse fluently in Navajo and, to a limited extent, several other languages. He enjoys listening to African pop music and has been, at various times, the only caucasian present at social gatherings of Asians, Hispanics, Blacks, and Indians. If this book sells far beyond his expectations, he will pay off his debts and take a trip to Greenland.

His hobbies include studying the martial arts and Chinese cooking.

About the Illustrator

Ted Kersten holds a degree in fine arts from Skidmore College. More than a free-lance graphics artist, he is also lead guitarist with Saucer, an alternative band that plays to highly select and highly appreciative audiences throughout the United States and which has put out a self-titled, full-length CD. Despite these lofty achievements and great talents, the sad fact is that he, too, makes his living as an overeducated security guard. He has no use for macho bullshit, but he does occasionally do things simply to see if they can be done. He's never written for magazines such as *Skeptic* or *Skeptical Inquirer* but insists that he probably could if he put his mind to it. He just doesn't want to because they're both pretty stuffy when you get right down to it. He shares the same birthday as Benito Mussolini and the famous author, Peter Huston.

About the Model, Creative Consultant, and Number One Hubcap Tosser

Lewis Treadway, of the famed international modeling agency "Chez Lewie," may not be the world's greatest model, but he comes cheap and is an amiable worker. Like Cindy Crawford, he has a birthmark and, like Naomi Campbell, he is rumored to be troublesome to work with, although he steadfastly denies it. He works in the retail of crafts supplies and has never had the least bit of desire to be a security guard. Although he disdains macho bullshit, the truth is that he once had an uncle whose cousin had a nephew in the administrative division of the Palestinian Liberation Organization (he's a quarter Palestinian by birth) and knows somebody who once knew somebody who had lunch with Steven Seagal, the martial arts movie star. He frequently does things. He is the librarian of the Inquiring Skeptics of Upper New York and has an amazing knowledge of TV trivia as well as several peculiar fields, including the literature of H.P. Lovecraft, Huey P. Long's life and career, Middle Eastern history, and more. He enjoys collecting and drinking wine. Despite the boyish looks, he is in his thirties. He is single, and women may write to him in care of the publisher.